D1617505

KNOWLEDGE AND FALLIBILISM

Essays on Improving Education

KNOWLEDGE AND FALLIBILISM:

Essays on Improving Education

RONALD M. SWARTZ
Associate Professor of Education
Oakland University
Rochester, Michigan

HENRY J. PERKINSON
Professor of History of Education
New York University
New York City

STEPHENIE G. EDGERTON
Professor of Educational Philosophy
New York University
New York City

New York and London · NEW YORK UNIVERSITY PRESS · 1980

Copyright © 1980 by New York University

Library of Congress Cataloging in Publication Data

Swartz, Ronald M.
  Knowledge and fallibilism.

  Bibliography: p.
  Includes index.
  1. Education—Philosophy. 2. Education—History—
20th century. I. Perkinson, Henry J., joint author.
II. Edgerton, Stephenie G., joint author. III. Title.
LB1025.S969   370.1   79-3068
ISBN 0-8147-7808-9

Manufactured in the United States of America

Contents

Acknowledgments

The authors would like to thank the following for granting permission to publish essays that have previously appeared in print: *The Cutting Edge, Focus on Learning, High School Journal*, International Reading Association, *Journal of Thought*, and *Social Education*. The three essays which appear as chapters 4, 5, and 6 were read at a session at the American Educational Studies Association Annual Meeting in Memphis, Tennessee, during November 1976. Our session at the AESA convention helped us all better understand our ideas about fallibilism, and we are grateful for the interest that was shown by a number of the association's members. Finally, it should be noted here that the works of Karl R. Popper and his followers have been the major intellectual influence on the ideas we develop throughout this book.

Ronald M. Swartz
Henry J. Perkinson
Stephenie G. Edgerton

Introduction:
Towards a Fallibilistic
Educational Perspective

RONALD SWARTZ

There is another intellectual use which philosophy ought to have, though in this respect it not infrequently fails. It ought to inculcate a realization of human fallibility and of the uncertainty of many things which to the uneducated seem indubitable.

—Bertrand Russell

... at the present time different sciences of education are not only possible but also much needed. Of course such a statement goes contrary to the idea that science by its very nature is a single and universal system of truths. But this idea need not frighten us. Even in the advanced sciences, like those of mathematics and physics, advance is made by entertaining different points of view and hypotheses, and working upon different theories. The sciences present no fixed and closed orthodoxy.

−John Dewey

. . . the belief in scientific certainty and in the authority of science is just wishful thinking: *science is fallible, because science is human.*

−Karl Popper

TWENTIETH-CENTURY FALLIBILISM AND PHILOSOPHY

Fallibilism is a rich and diversified intellectual tradition which includes such twentieth-century Western philosophers as Bertrand Russell (1872–1967), John Dewey (1859–1952), and Karl Popper (1902–).[1] Although fallibilists existed before this century, it was only after Albert Einstein (1879–1955) showed that Isaac Newton (1642–1727) had not discovered the absolute truth about the workings of the universe that modern philosophers started to draw theoretical and practical implications from the notion that scientific knowledge—even all human ideas and beliefs—may eventually be shown to be mistaken. It is hard for us moderns to realize that some peoples living in earlier times thought they possessed the absolute truth about the universe; incredible as it might seem to us, many scientists in the eighteenth and nineteenth centuries believed that Newton's theories were absolutely true. Of his, Leopold Infeld has noted:

The celebrated mathematician Lagrange, who died in the early nineteenth century, remarked that Newton was not only the greatest but the most fortunate among scientists, because the science of our world can be created only once, and it was Newton who created it. From our present vantage point, it is clear that the foundations of science have been created and re-created and that Newton's great achievement was the creation of only the first link in a chain of scientific revolutions. Nevertheless, when Lagrange lived, and even later, almost throughout the first half of the nineteenth century, the mechanical view [developed by Newton] spread and deepened until it assumed the status of a philosophical dogma. . . .

In those times, scientists assumed that our entire universe, and we in it, form a gigantic complicated machine that obeys Newtonian laws.[2]

Later in this introduction more will be said about how twentieth-century science has affected the development of a fallibilistic view of human knowledge. Here it is important to understand that fallibilism is a philosophical perspective which rests on the assumption that people can never be certain that their ideas or beliefs are absolutely true. For a fallibilist, all that is known today will very likely be superseded by very different and potentially better ideas. Just as Newtonian physics was revolutionized by Einstein's theories about the universe, it is quite possible to envision a new physics that will render the ideas developed by Einstein relatively obsolete.

An account of all the possible views associated with fallibilism would not entail a clearly defined body of ideas that all fallibilists had agreed upon. On the contrary, a comprehensive history of fallibilism would encompass the many disputes and disagreements which have existed between those who were willing to admit that all human ideas may someday be improved. Consider the work of Russell and Dewey: although these philosophers had much in common, they did in some respects endorse entirely different ideas. One of the most important debates in twentieth-century Western philosophy concerns the question of how to view truth. Russell argued that truth should be viewed as an absolute and unchanging entity, whereas Dewey and such leading pragmatists as William James (1842–1910) and Charles S. Peirce (1839–1914) suggested that truth could be seen as an entity which changes over time.

This is not the occasion to examine various fallibilistic perspectives in detail. This introduction and the chapters that follow are intended to provide a beginning attempt at understanding the relevance of fallibilism for contemporary life and schooling. Of all modern philosophies, the work of Karl R. Popper has had the greatest intellectual influence on the three authors of this volume. Particularly influential on these essays are Popper's ideas on fallibilism, science, and the growth of knowledge and institutions. In common with other fallibilists, the authors do not agree with one another about all issues concerning fallibilism, learning, and schooling; readers will find some important disagreements among them.

FALLIBILISM AND THE ROLE OF PROBLEMS IN HUMAN UNDERSTANDING

To attain an understanding of fallibilism, it is necessary to consider the central role of problems within the fallibilistic tradition. Let us now consider what some fallibilists have said about problems.

The careful reader will quickly note that all of the chapters center around the asking of questions or the attempts to solve problems (the terms "question" and "problem" are used interchangeably throughout this book). That is, every question can be viewed as a problem which can be solved by a number of answers.

It is not accidental that the three authors of this volume have decided to emphasize problems in their attempts to better understand educational issues, since they believe that questions and problems are a central part of the human quest for knowledge and understanding. In addition, readers will see that none of the authors makes a claim to have the final answers to the questions raised. At best, the answers suggested are given in the hope of trying to direct attention to important problems so that a more satisfactory dialogue about educational issues will develop in future educational discussions. In other words, the authors are fallibilists themselves and do not treat fallibilism simply as a viable intellectual perspective. Fallibilism as it is discussed in this introduction should be applied to the chapters which follow; all the knowledge claims made in this book are tentative. Hopefully, the ideas suggested will eventually be superseded by other questions and views which will help human beings better understand how to use their educational institutions.

Although fallibilists are likely to emphasize the importance of problems, it is worth noting that the quest for knowledge does not always start with a question that has been clearly stated; sometimes people have to think or write for awhile before they become fully aware of the problems they are dealing with. Of course, an individual may have a vague awareness of a question before he is able to articulate it, but one can *share* problems with others only if and when one can *state a problem as a question.* The thought processes must be translated into a *verbal context* to make ideas open to criticism and public discussion. However, the verbal expression of a problem might not adequately or accurately identify the specific question one wishes to answer, since the articulation of a problem is in one sense a conjecture about the question one wants to ask. As is true of all conjectures, individuals may have a mistaken idea about the problem they wish to solve; many people have written about one problem while claiming to be concerned with another.

Although human beings have at times been confused about their ideas, some fallibilists have nevertheless decided that human understanding can be greatly aided when people articulate the questions they wish to have answered; when a group of individuals study a question it can generally be viewed from more than one perspective. No matter how much we may think one answer to a question is true, there is usually someone who opts for a different answer from ours. The study of problems necessitates the consideration of diverse points of view because it is a simple fact that people can and often do disagree with one another about the best answer to a given question.

Since fallibilists are always willing to admit that their best conjecture about how to solve a problem may in fact be false, they rely on the use of questions as a way to contrast alternative viewpoints. Naturally, fallibilists also emphasize questions when discussing the improvement and growth of knowledge; that is, we can say that knowledge has "improved" if we can demonstrate that an old answer to a question is not as good as a new answer. It may not be easy to decide if one answer to a question is better than another; many fallibilists may disagree about which known answer to a question is indeed the best one. Nevertheless, the articulation of questions helps to structure discussions in such a way that *competing* ideas can be evaluated and criticized in the hope of improving understanding.

A second major idea to understand in regard to problems is that the question (or questions) used to articulate a problem can help us comprehend the intellectual or theoretical framework in which the question is rooted. The questions people raise always imply a number of explicit and implicit assumptions; hence, they provide clues to the assumptions and ideas individuals endorse. Specifically, if a person were to ask the question, "How do wings make it possible for birds to fly?" it can be said that the questioner assumes that birds have wings which make flying possible. In addition, the assumptions underlying questions may be either true or false. And some questions rely on mistaken or inadequate notions. "How do wings make it possible for *snakes* to fly?" is an example of a problem which makes a mistaken assumption. Most of us would probably not wish to discuss how wings help snakes to fly.

When human knowledge is viewed as the study of problem situations, it is desirable to analyze the assumptions implicit in the questions asked. Although we may never be able to articulate all the assumptions people make, it is important to identify the crucial or important assumptions associated with our questions. If one does not critically evaluate the assumptions to a question, dialogues may center on meaningless and trivial issues. Unfortunately, many people have spent years trying to answer questions similar to the one about flying snakes. If we reflect on our questions, we may be able to avoid unproductive dialogues.

The third important point in this regard is that it is impossible ever to have complete understanding of all the assumptions associated with any one question: all questions have an incalculable number of assumptions associated with them; every idea, assumption, or statement implies an *infinite* number of other ideas. This assertion suggests that human understanding can never be perfect. It is always possible to give a greater and deeper explanation about what we mean. Put differently, our ability to comprehend any idea is *limited*, because human language is structured in such a way that every statement is dependent upon more ideas than anyone could articulate in a lifetime. In regard to this notion, Karl Popper once wrote the following:

> when we propose a theory, or try to understand a theory, we also propose, or try to understand, its logical implications; that is, all those statements which follow from it. But this . . . is a hopeless task: there is an *infinity of unforeseeable non-trivial statements belonging to the informative content of any theory*, and an exactly corresponding infinity of statements belonging to its logical content. We can therefore never know or understand all the implications of any theory, or its full significance.[3]

One of the foundational ideas of various forms of fallibilism is that *all human statements have an infinite number of assumptions associated with them.* Although it may be very difficult to imagine that every idea depends upon an infinite number of other ideas, this notion is readily understandable when we consider the fact that it is always possible to give a more detailed explanation of our thoughts and a more precise definition of the words we use. Of course, broader explanations or more definitions are certainly not needed to convey a general understanding of our thoughts in many, especially ordinary situations. Fortunately for human beings, communication does not depend on having a perfect understanding of any statement or concept.

Fallibilists endorse the view that human beings can never have a perfect understanding or any question, theory, or statement. Too, the inability ever to totally understand our ideas suggests that people must learn to be *selective* when they attempt to understand any idea or question. Once we realize that we cannot know everything there is to know about any qeustion, we must learn how to distinguish the important assumptions and ideas from the trivial, insignificant ones. For example, an important assumption associated with the question, "How do wings make it possible for snakes to fly?" is the assumption that snakes have wings. This assumption is crucial, since any dialogue about snakes flying would rely on the notion that snakes have wings. Thus, although fallibilists can admit that human understanding is never perfect, they can make judgments about what questions or problems are worthy of consideration.

A fourth issue to emphasize about questions is that the change from one problem situation to another may at times be judged as progressive. A *progressive problem shift* occurs when one question is superseded by another that makes more satisfactory assumptions. Changing the question, "How do wings make it possible for snakes to fly?" to the question, "How do the muscles in the body of snakes make it possible for snakes to crawl?" is a progressive problem shift. The replacement of the first question by the second one is progressive if one accepts the fact that snakes do not have wings.

When two or more questions compete for our attention, it is often possible to decide which question is the more satisfactory one: the question worth considering is the one which makes the most satisfactory assumptions. Thus, an evaluation of competing questions often demonstrates that some questions are more satisfactory than others, although not all individuals may agree about which assumptions are indeed the most satisfactory. In fact, many debates about the best question to ask and work on are not conclusive, since different groups of people somtimes offer competing evaluations of the assumptions made by the questions being discussed.

It is often quite difficult to decide if the change from one question to another is actually progressive. Nevertheless, fallibilists have often noted that human knowledge improves as people learn to shift their problem situations. In regard to how progress can be judged by the questions asked, John Dewey once wrote:

> intellectual progress usually occurs through sheer abandonment of questions. . . . Old questions are solved by disappearing, evaporating, while new questions corresponding to changed attitudes of endeavor and preference take their place.[4]

It should now be fairly clear why some fallibilists have spent so much time studying the importance of questions in the human quest for understanding. To summarize, the following four ideas about problems have been discussed in this section: (1) the quest for knowledge and an improved understanding of the world is greatly aided by attempts to articulate problems as questions; (2) the questions we use to state our problems are important because these questions give clues to the assumptions and ideas people endorse; (3) it is impossible ever to have a total awareness of all the assumptions associated with any single question, because all questions rely upon an infinite number of assumptions; and (4) intellectual progress and the growth of human knowledge can at times be realized by a shift from one problem situation to another.

CENTRAL PROBLEM OF THE BOOK—NEED FOR A HISTORY OF FALLIBILISM

This introduction, and the papers which follow, attempt to ask and answer the following question: How is a fallibilistic view of human knowledge and human activity relevant for schooling?

This question is quite general, and the essays in this volume attempt to outline some of the specific aspects of a fallibilistic educational philosophy. Nevertheless, this book does not contain a comprehensive statement about a fallibilistic educational perspective. Rather, this volume marks a beginning attempt to draw some educational implications from recent developments within the fallibilistic tradition, and the specific papers give only hints at the possible directions of our thinking if we wish to attain a fallibilistic educational perspective.

All of the chapters were written to stand by themselves. Each one centers on one particular aspect of a fallibilistic educational perspective. However, there are some common themes all of the authors endorse. These common themes reflect a shared historical view of fallibilism, which guides the philosophical perspective endorsed throughout this work.

In order to gain an understanding of a fallibilistic educational perspective, one needs to know the problems, questions, and ideas which have led people to view all human knowledge and activities as imperfect and improvable. The history of fallibilism is an account of the growing awareness that human beings, despite the fact that they can at times invent ingenious ideas, can never be perfect or know that what they believe is absolutely true. As we have said, fallibilists disagree about many issues, but what separates fallibilists from those with other views on the nature of knowledge and the nature of man is that they are willing to admit that human understanding is limited and imperfect. For fallibilists, the knowledge or beliefs of any given period may well be superseded by new and better ideas at a later time.

Fallibilism has developed into a modern Western philosophical perspective which has many fascinating variations. With respect to education, the fallibilistic views of contemporary thinkers such as Karl Popper suggest that educational theories and practices need to be altered. Unfortunately, social institutions, including schools, often rely on ideas that lag behind current philosophical developments; thus, an outline of the history of fallibilism may help close the gap between modern philosophy and contemporary educational thought and provide a better understanding of the relevance of fallibilistic ideas to schooling and learning. With the aim of understanding how the ideas presented in this book evolved from recent discoveries within the fallibilistic tradition, let us begin by sketching a history of modern versions of fallibilism.

THE DEVELOPMENT OF PRAGMATISM FROM MILL TO DEWEY

A history of fallibilism can begin with a discussion of the question, "What should be the goal of scientific inquiry?" This question, which we can refer to as *the problem of the aim of science*, has been answered differently by fallibilists such as Dewey and Popper. Popper's brand of fallibilism suggests that it is desirable to view the human quest for knowledge as an infinite and continuous dialogue which attempts to get closer to the *unattainable goal of absolute truth*; for Popperian fallibilists, all questions have an absolutely true answer, but human beings can never know if the answer they endorse at any moment in time is indeed the truth. On the other hand, pragmatists like Dewey helped to develop a new view of truth, which holds that truth *changes* from time to time. This section attempts to explain how pragmatic fallibilism came to develop a new view of truth.

John Stuart Mill (1806–73), Charles Sanders Peirce, William James, and John Dewey are four great fallibilists who were in great part responsible for developing the modern philosophy of pragmatism. American pragmatism, and the pragmatic view of truth, has its historical roots in the work of John Stuart Mill, but unfortunately the connection between Mill and the American pragmatists is often forgotten. William James, however, was very much aware of his intellectual debt to Mill; James's dedication to his famous essay called "Pragmatism" (1907) states:

To the memory of John Stuart Mill from whom I first learned the pragmatic openness of mind and whom my fancy likes to picture as our leader were he alive today.[5]

Although Mill wrote and lived when Newton's scientific theories were considered to be the absolute truth, Mill was not one to be impressed with success or public opinion. Mill was an independent thinker, and in 1859 he had the courage to write the following:

The beliefs which we have most warrant for, have no safeguard to rest on, but a standing invitation to the whole world to prove them unfounded. If the challenge is not accepted, or is accepted and the attempts fail, we are far enough from certainty still; but we have done the best that the existing state of human reason admits of; we have neglected nothing that could give the truth a chance of reaching us: if the lists are kept open, we may hope that if there is a better truth, it will be found when the human mind is capable of receiving it; and in the meantime we may rely on having attained such approach to truth, as is possible in our own day. This is the amount of cretainty attainable by a fallible being, and this the sole way of attaining it.[6]

Mill's views on human fallibility and the method for approaching truth have directness and simplicity. In many ways Mill's ideas seem so reasonable that it is difficult to see that his fallibilistic philosophy was a significant break with the reigning ideas of the nineteenth century. A major reason that many people today find it difficult to understand why Mill's ideas were not well received by his contemporaries is that we live in the post-Einsteinian era, and it seems self-evident to moderns that scientific theories are no longer viewed as perfect and absolutely true. Of course, Mill lived well before Einstein, when it was seemed equally self-evident that mankind had discovered the "truth," [7] and nineteenth-century individuals were therefore impatient with philosophers such as Mill who could not see the simple "fact" that Newton had already discovered absolute truth.

Why is it that John Stuart Mill developed his ideas on fallibilism at a time when Newtonian theories were virtually totally accepted? The answer to this question requires some familiarity with the work of the British philosopher David Hume (1711–76). Hume's views about human knowledge and the scientific method will be discussed later in this introduction; here, it is sufficient to note that Hume developed arguments which clearly showed that *no empirical idea* could be demonstrated to be absolutely true, because there was always the possibility that some future experience would contradict a theory that has been supported by past experiences.[8]

Hume's ideas about empirical knowledge and the scientific method have been a thorn in the side of later philosophers. The literature on Hume's epistomological views is voluminous, and his work is often seen as causing a crisis for theoretical science. If one accepts Hume's arguments that some future experiences might contradict what we know, it becomes necessary to admit that known scientific ideas may be false. Mill was well acquainted with Hume's theories, and consequently, despite the tremendous success of Newton's scientific theories, he remembered what Hume had said about not being able to know with certainty that man's ideas could indeed be absolutely true.

The pragmatic branch of the fallibilistic tradition had other nineteenth-century advocates besides Mill. Charles Sanders Peirce, an astute American philosopher, was also familiar with Hume's arguments. In 1896 in his well-known essay called "The Scientific Attitude and Fallibilism" Peirce wrote the following:

we cannot in any way reach perfect certitude nor exactitude. We never can be absolutely sure of anything. . . . I believe I may say there is no tenable opinion regarding human knowledge which does not legitimately lead to this corollary. Certainly there is nothing new in it; and many of the greatest minds of all time have held it for true.

Indeed, most everyone will admit it until he begins to see what is involved in the admission—and then most people will draw back. It will not be admitted by persons utterly incapable of philosophical reflection. It will not be admitted by masterful minds developed exclusively in the direction of action and accustomed to claim practical infallibility in matters of business. These men will admit the incurable fallibility of all opinions readily enough; only, they will always make exceptions of their own.[9]

Peirce, like Mill, developed his fallibilistic philosophy before Einstein developed his revolutionary scientific theories. But Peirce died before the scientific community could recover from the shock that Newton's theories were not absolutely true but were an *approximation* of the truth, and thus it was left to those who followed Peirce to develop a pragmatic philosophy which could account for the fact that scientific theories, no matter how well supported by experience, should be viewed as imperfect and fallible.

One of the most famous pragmatists who did much of his work in the post-Einsteinian era is John Dewey. Born in 1859, Dewey lived to the age of ninety-three. Throughout most of his life he remained intellectually active, and when he was seventy years old his well-known book, *The Quest for Certainty*, was published. This work is important in part because it was written in the post-Einsteinian era. By 1929 Dewey was fully aware of the impact of Einstein's discoveries on man's views on scientific theories. In *The Quest for Certainty*, Dewey wrote:

even if the details of the Einstein theory of relativity should be some time discredited, a genuine revolution, and one

which will not go backward, has been effected in the theory of
the origin, nature, and test of scientific ideas.[10]

Today Dewey is primarily remembered as a philosopher of education, and his books in the philosophy of science have not received as much attention as his educational works. Nevertheless,
Dewey's views on science and the scientific method constitute
some of his most important contributions to the world of scholar-
ship. Furthermore, the study of Dewey's writings on the philosophy of science can greatly enrich one's understanding of his
philosophy of education. In fact, Dewey's pragmatic philosophy of
education applies a pragmatic philosophy of science to the educational process. Thus, one can gain a greater understanding of
Dewey's views of the aim of inquiry in an educational program by
turning first to his works on science and the scientific method. For
Dewey, the aim of inquiry in a classroom was the *same* as the aim
of inquiry in science. In this connection, Dewey wrote the following:

> scientific method provides a working pattern of the way in
> which and the conditions under which experiences are used to
> lead ever onward and outward. Adaptation of the method to
> individuals of various degrees of maturity is a problem for the
> educator, and the constant factors in the problem are the
> formation of ideas, acting upon ideas, observation of the con-
> ditions which result, and organization of facts and ideas for
> future use.[11]

Since Dewey developed his pragmatic views after the scientific
discoveries of Einstein, he did not encounter the kind of opposition Mill and Peirce had had to face. After Einstein it became
possible for many people to understand that scientific theories
could change over time. To Dewey's credit, he attempted to develop a philosophy of science which would not allow Einstein's
ideas to become a new scientific dogma—he realized that at some
future date even Einstein's theories might be superseded (a lesson
learned from the thrust of the Einsteinian revolution itself). But
after Einstein, it was necessary for Dewey to view old problems in

a new light. For example, Dewey realized he had to reconsider the traditional answer to questions such as, "What should be the goal of scientific inquiry?" Before Einstein's discoveries were made, most individuals thought that absolute truth should be the aim of science. After the Einsteinian revolution, people began to wonder about whether it was reasonable for scientists to continue to search for absolute truth.

Dewey's answer to the question of the aim of science followed in the footsteps of Peirce. Dewey suggested that scientific theories could never be absolutely true; instead, he endorsed the notion that *the truth of all scientific theories was relative to what is known at any moment in time.* If at some future time scientists should discover new evidence contradicting what was believed to be a scientific truth, then that "truth" would have to be replaced with a new "truth." In other words, for Dewey, Newton's theories were true during the pre-Einstein age; but after Einstein, scientific communities could no longer call Newton's ideas true, since scientists had discovered new experiences which suggested that Einstein's views gave more satisfactory explanations to scientific questions than Newton's theories did.

Much has been written about the pragmatic view of truth, and it would be inappropriate in this introduction to discuss the many fascinating issues that have arisen from what Dewey and the other pragmatists have said about the aim of scientific inquiry. However, for our purposes, it is important to note that as late as 1938 Dewey still held to the view that *truth was merely an opinion held by a community of scientists,* and he maintained his belief that this opinion could change in the light of new evidence. In a famous footnote in *Logic: The Theory of Inquiry,* Dewey wrote the following:

> The best definition of *truth* from the logical standpoint which is known to me is that of Peirce: "The opinion which is fated to be ultimately agreed to by all who investigate is what we mean by the truth, and the object represented by this opinion is the real." [12]

THE RUSSELL-POPPER CRITIQUE OF PRAGMATIC TRUTH

Pragmatist views regarding truth were not accepted by all twentieth-century fallibilists. Such fallibilists as Bertrand Russell and Karl Popper have argued against the notion that a pragmatic or relative truth was the aim of science. Let us now consider why some fallibilists rejected the pragmatists' answer to the problem of the aim of science.

In regard to Dewey's ideas, Russell once wrote the following:

Dr. Dewey's world, it seems to me, is one in which human beings occupy the imagination; the cosmos of astronomy, though of course acknowledged to exist, is at most times ignored. His philosophy is a power philosophy, though not, like Nietzsche's, a philosophy of individual power; it is the power of the community that is felt to be valuable. . . .

In all this I feel a grave danger, the danger of what might be called cosmic impiety. The concept of "truth" as something dependent upon facts largely outside human control has been one of the ways in which philosophy hitherto has inculcated the necessary element of humility. When this check upon pride is removed, a further step is taken on the road towards a certain kind of madness—the intoxication of power which invaded philosophy with Fichte, and to which modern men, whether philosophers or not, are prone. I am persuaded that this intoxication is the greatest danger of our time, and that any philosophy which, however unintentionally, contributes to it is increasing the danger of vast social disaster.[13]

In their efforts to solve the problem of the aim of science, Russell and Popper are more traditional than Dewey and the other pragmatists. Russell and Popper wanted to maintain that science attempts to discover the absolute truth about the world we live in, as did Hume and, in some respects, a number of Western philosophers who lived before Plato (427–327 B.C.). As we have already indicated, *the pragmatists were willing to relinquish the long-es-tablished idea of viewing absolute truth as the aim of science;* furthermore, they conceived the radical idea that science itself had a new aim. Thus, they endorsed the fallibilists' notion that what is thought to be true today might be shown to be false tomorrow. However, pragmatists also thought that scientific in-quiry had long periods of stability, and they were willing to say that during such periods those ideas which were warranted or ver-ified by the known facts were to be viewed as "true" for the time being.

Russell and Popper both held that it is a mistake to give up the quest for absolute truth; these fallibilists have sought to retain this traditional aim of science. However, given what Hume had con-vincingly demonstrated about man's *inability* to prove that an idea is absolutely true, and in light of Einstein's discoveries, how could this seemingly untenable proposition be maintained? Rus-sell's and Popper's answer was that absolute truth should be viewed as the *unattainable* and never ending goal of scientific inquiry. In this regard, Popper wrote:

> the task of science is the search for truth, that is, for true theories (even though as Xenophanes pointed out we may never get them, or know them *as true* if we get them). Yet we also stress that *truth is not the only aim of science.* We want more than mere truth: what we look for is *interesting truth—* truth which is hard to come by. . . . Mere truth is not enough; what we look for are *answers to our problems.*[14]

To say that absolute truth is an unattainable goal that we can strive for but never attain suggests that the complete truth is *in-comprehensible and infinite*: all ideas can always be enlarged and expanded to include more information or content. For example, in trying to discover the truth about the color of swans one might suggest the proposition, "All swans are white." Even if this state-ment were true, one could claim that it is not absolutely and completely true, because it does not take into account how vari-ous light waves might affect the color of swans. Thus, some of our ideas might be *partly* true, or contain true aspects, but no idea can be absolutely true, because *we can always conjecture a more informative theory that might contain more of the truth.* If we accept the view, discussed earlier, that all ideas have an *infinite* number of assumptions associated with them, then no statement or verbal account of an idea can contain the complete truth, since it is always possible to *further* explain any theory. Some ideas may be partly true, but no ideas can be absolutely true, because there are always some aspects of all ideas which must remain unknown. Also, since absolute truth is never attained, human understanding can always be impoved: what we know at any moment in time may eventually be superseded by new and better ideas.

In contemporary philosophical circles it is fairly common to say that absolute truth is unattainable, but it is *uncommon* to recommend that people continue to strive for an unattainable truth. Many present-day philosophers have suggested that it is more reasonable to strive for attainable goals, such as theories with a high probability. However, it can be considered both reasonable and desirable to strive for unattainable goals, such as absolute truth. In any case, it is obvious that there is a sharp distinction between pragmatism and the philosophies of science developed by Russell and Popper.

Russell's views on truth were not readily accepted by Dewey and later pragmatist philosophers. Philosophical debates about important problems related to truth are not easily decided, and philosophers can usually find a way to answer their critics. For our purposes it is not necessary to consider the issues which divide Dewey, Russell, and Popper in great detail; what is significant in the present context is that modern philosophers *disagree* about how to best solve the problem of the aim of science. The authors of this book have more in common with Popper than with Dewey: they attempt to view educational problems from the perspective of Popperian fallibilism rather than from the point of view of pragmatic fallibilism, a viewpoint espoused by numerous other contemporary educational theorists.

The papers presented here draw educational implications from the idea that absolute truth should be the aim of scientific inquiry. Many of Popper's ideas related to viewing inquiry as a continuous dialogue which aims at discovering absolute truth are

discussed in the chapters "Authority, Responsibility, and Democratic Schooling"; "Against Learning"; and "Skepticism and
Schooling." These chapters, as well as some of the others, attempt
to point out that the teacher's knowledge, as well as the ideas
included in the usual school curriculum, should not be viewed
either as final or as pragmatic truths; all of the authors present
their views about how teachers and students should engage in a
continuous dialogue to solve problems and approach the unattainable goal of absolute truth. The goal of absolute truth as the
aim of research directed toward a better understanding of the
educational process also receives some attention.

Let us conclude this section with an account of some of the
significant points made to this point about fallibilism and the
problem of the aim of science. The following major points have
been suggested: (1) The fallibilism of Dewey and the other pragmatists can be distinguished from the fallibilistic philosophies of
Russell and Popper because the latter two twentieth-century
thinkers opted to view absolute and infinite truth as the unattainable but legitimate aim of science. (2) Although some wish to
minimize the differences between Popperian fallibilism and pragmatic fallibilism, these differences may prove to have profound
theoretical and practical consequences for the study of educational problems. (3) Fallibilists such as Russell and Popper have
argued that without an objective standard such as truth or falsity
by which to judge our ideas, we may be forced into a position
which allows the truth of an idea to be determined by power
politics rather than by rational means. Such a position is unaccept-
able to many fallibilists in that they wish to associate fallibilism
with a theory of rationality which is not reduced to a struggle for
power. (4) The quest for absolute truth is viewed by Russell and
Popper as one way to allow for constant improvement. Fallibilists
who seek an unattainable goal such as absolute truth do not do so
because they wish to frustrate people; instead, this goal is meant
to encourage people to seek improvement constantly. (5) Finally,
fallibilists such as Russell and Popper have suggested that the
quest for unattainable truth allows people to avoid being authoritarian or self-righteous about the ideas they know at any given
moment. Although some persons may believe that their ideas are

better or less flawed than those of others, the fallibilistic philosophies of Russell and Popper encourage *all* individuals to strive for
improvement, since no one can claim to know the absolute truth.

HUME'S VIEW OF INDUCTION; EMPIRICAL THEORIES

The difference between Popperian fallibilism and pragmatic fallibilism is quite important for an understanding of how this book
fits into the contemporary literature related to educational problems. In contemporary educational circles, the influence of the
pragmatists has been immense. No contemporary educational theorist or practitioner can ignore John Dewey's work and the work of
his disciples such as William H. Kilpatrick (1871–1965). Thus, if
one wishes to have a meaningful dialogue about existing educational theories and institutions, one must take into account what
the pragmatists have said and done: to ignore the pragmatists is
akin to sticking one's head in the sand. Also, any changes in our
ideas about educational theory and practice must take into account the views of Dewey and the other pragmatists.

Twentieth-century fallibilism, as we can now readily see, has
developed *competing* formulations. As will become clearer in sub-
sequent sections, in part because Dewey, Russell, and Popper do
not entirely agree with one another about how science operates,
contemporary fallibilism has been greatly affected by *alternative*
views of the scientific method. But before discussing different
twentieth-century versions of fallibilism, it is necessary to comment further on the eighteenth-century philosopher David
Hume's ideas, particularly those relating to the scientific method
per se.

Most recent versions of fallibilism have had to deal with
Hume's ideas about the fact that no amount of positive evidence
can justify that an empirical idea is absolutely true. Hume was
deeply concerned with trying to understand how knowledge, especially scientific knowledge, could be justified by experience. For
Hume, it was extremely important to answer a question such as,
"How can experience demonstrate and justify that our ideas, and

particularly scientific theories, are absolutely true and certain?" This question, which we can refer to as *the Humian problem of induction,* seemed to have greatly troubled Hume. Hume's suring solution to his problem—about the validity of an empirical method—was that experience *cannot* demonstrate that scientific theories or any universal statements are indeed true. Hume argued that no amount of positive evidence could justify the truthfulness of a universal statement such as "All swans are white" because he realized that universal statements imply something about the future. He pointed out that what we have experienced in the past may not hold in the future:

> Let men be once fully persuaded of these two principles, *that there is nothing in any object, considered in itself, which can afford us a reason for drawing a conclusion beyond it;* and, *that even after the observation of frequent or constant conjunction of objects, we have no reason to draw any inference concerning any objects beyond those of which we have had experience.*[15]

Hume reached these conclusions after much soul-searching. He held that inductive reasoning (reasoning based upon inferences from specific experiences leading to universal statements) could *never* result in propositions or theories that could be justified or demonstrated to be true. Put another way, Hume decided that inductive inferences, conclusions based upon the accumulation of many similar experiences, could never be known to be absolutely true. And in spite of what Aristotle (384–322 B.C.), Francis Bacon (1561–1626), and all the other great inductivists have said about the role of induction in science, Hume's conclusion was that induction could not demonstrate that scientific ideas were true. Although he noted that people could continue to believe in the principle of induction, he suggested that this principle could not be justified by experience or reason.

Here a brief word about the difference between inductive and deductive reasoning is in order. These two different modes of reasoning are often confused with one another, but they are quite

different. In deduction, one reasons from known premises to conclusions which are already contained within these premises. For
example, a famous deduction is the following:

1. All men are mortal. (first premise)
2. Socrates is a man. (second premise)
3. Therefore, Socrates is mortal. (deductive conclusion)

In this deduction the third statement or conclusion is *implied by
or contained within* the first two statements. That is, the third
statement does *not* say anything new but *combines* what is said in
the first two statements. In addition, truth can be transferred from
premises to a conclusion if one draws a conclusion that is indeed
implied by the premises. Of course, the problem is that when one
uses deductive reasoning, the truthfulness of premises may not be
known, and if this is the case it is wrong to assume that conclusions are true. In any case, one can always decide if a conclusion is
indeed implied in certain premises. An example of a legitimate
deduction that appears to draw a false conclusion is the following:

1. All snakes can fly.
2. There is a snake in my garden today.
3. Therefore, the snake in my garden can fly.

This deduction about flying snakes is a legitimate use of deductive
reasoning because the conclusion merely combines what is stated
in the premises. Thus, deductive reasoning is simply a logical technique that allows one to draw conclusions from known statements.
When conclusions are legitimately drawn, they simply state information that is *contained within the premises*.

Inductive reasoning is very different from deductive reasoning
because inductive reasoning is based on the attempt to make inferences which contain information that goes *beyond* what is
implied in the original premises; unlike deduction, inductive reasoning attempts to draw conclusions which are not contained
within one's premises. An example of an inductive inference is the
following:

1. There is a white swan in the park today. (first premise)
2. There was a white swan in the zoo yesterday. (second premise)
3. There was a white swan in my backyard a week ago. (third premise)
4. Therefore, all swans are white. (inductive conclusion)

The conclusion is *not contained in or implied by* the first three statements, and the conclusion says something *more* than is in the premises. Furthermore, unlike deductive reasoning, it cannot be claimed that inductive conclusions are truth if one's premises are true; even if one's premises are true, a conclusion could be false because inductive inferences say *more* than what is contained within one's original premises.

Hume was primarily interested in inductive reasoning and did not attempt to criticize the basic principles of deductive reasoning. And since Hume's time it has been very difficult for anyone to claim that induction could be used to demonstrate the truthfulness of scientific theories. In a sense, then, Hume's views on induction created a crisis in science, mentioned briefly earlier. Once a person endorses Hume's critique of induction, rather than attempting to refute it or show it to be wrong, one must accept the view that scientific theories—no matter how successful they may be—can never be accepted as absolute truths.

Once Hume had laid out his devastating critique of induction in the eighteenth century, on the face of it the reasonable thing to do was to *stop* believing that inductive inferences were true. But what seems rational and reasonable is not what people always do. Furthermore, given the tremendous success of science, particularly of Newton's ideas, it is understandable that many scientists and philosophers thought that the process of induction did indeed demonstrate that scientific theories were true. Eighteenth- and nineteenth-century scholars were very optimistic about science and the ability of scientists to discover the truth.[16] It is hard for us today, in our technological world, to imagine that science was successful hundreds of years ago, since we often tend to look at the past and think that people did not really know very much.

However, Newton's explanations about the universe were so valid within their limits that they even made possible the prediction of the existence of the planet Neptune before men had observed this planet. Thus, Newtonian ideas were able to predict *unobservable* events, and this fact could serve to reinforce people's belief that Newton's theories were absolutely true. Hume's arguments regarding induction could be used to demonstrate that Newtonian scientific theories were potentially fallible, but in light of the observable, highly convincing success of Newton's theories it must have seemed a bit silly to be doubtful. Thus, although it was, strictly speaking, unreasonable to claim that Newton's ideas were absolutely true, many scientists and philosophers thought that Newton had indeed discovered absolutely true theories.

In the interest of brevity, the foregoing account of induction and science in the eighteenth and nineteenth centuries has been necessarily very sketchy, and hence is somewhat distorted. Except for Mill, nothing has been said about those philosophers who continued to worry about the Humian problem of induction. If we were to present a more complete picture of eighteenth- and nineteenth-century science it would be necessary to discuss how Michael Faraday (1791–1867) attempted to develop alternative theories which challenged Newtonian scientific explanations. Also it would be necessary to consider the work of philosophers such as Immanuel Kant (1724–1804) who, like John Stuart Mill, took Hume's arguments very seriously.

The story about the place of induction in the history of Western philosophy would not be complete without a detailed account of the heroic efforts made by Kant and Mill to explain that inductive inferences could justify the truthfulness of scientific ideas. But here is not the place to give the details about the important role played by induction and science in the development of Western philosophical thought. Let us just say that the eventual failure to view induction as a reliable means to demonstrate the truth, coupled with the overthrow of Newtonian science by the Einsteinian revolution, made it necessary for Western philosophy to enter the twentieth century confronting the fact that even science and induction cannot be relied upon to demonstrate that any idea is true.

Given this state of affairs, both scientists and philosophers began to see the need to develop a philosophy of science that would allow scientific ideas to evolve and change as human awareness and imagination expanded. Also, since scientific ideas were no longer viewed as absolutely true, they were, in time, considered to be potentially fallible and improvable, since at any moment known theories might be shown to be false or inferior to yet undiscovered hypotheses.

EFFECT OF HUME'S CRITIQUE ON TWENTIETH-CENTURY THEORIES OF RATIONALITY

This introduction began with a discussion of the views of Bertrand Russel, John Dewey, and Karl Popper. Here we will explain how these twentieth-century philosophers developed views about science and the scientific method.

Russell, Dewey, and Popper can all be viewed as belonging to the rationalist group of fallibilists. That is, these philosophers tried to develop a philosophical perspective that in one way or another rests on the assumption that the use of reason, rather than faith alone, is crucial for human action and decision making. If we put aside the many areas of disagreement among Russell, Dewey, and Popper, it can be said that each of these men have favored the development of an intellectual framework that views reason as being quite important for human beings and consequently that it should play a significant role in human activities.

However, fallibilists have offered different recommendations about how human beings should cope with the basic inability to know the truth. For example, the assumption that human beings cannot know the absolute truth could be used as the basis for the development of irrationalist forms of fallibilism. And some fallibilists did become disillusioned with rationalism; at times fallibilists have even advocated belief in any idea for any reason, rational or irrational. In other words, fallibilism has led a number of people to recommend belief at all costs because some have thought that it would be too painful to live in a world where all ideas were viewed as uncertain and changeable. For example, the existentialist philosopher Miguel de Unamuno (1864–1936) seems to recommend that human beings should replace reason with faith. Unamuno was very much aware of Hume's critique of induction, and he once noted the following:

> The rational dissolution ends in dissolving reason itself; it ends in the most absolute scepticism, in the phenomenalism of Hume. . . . The supreme triumph of reason, the analytical—that is, the destructive and dissolvent—faculty, is to cast doubt upon its own validity. The stomach that contains an ulcer ends by digesting itself.[17]

In many of his writings Unamuno argues that faith should replace reason as a means for discovering good or true ideas. Although he does not argue that all decisions based on faith will necessarily be true or good, he does seem to suggest that the rationalists such as Hume have left man with no choice but to live by faith rather than by reason. Unamuno offers Don Quixote as the model for individuals to emulate; for Unamuno, human beings would be wise to follow Quixote's example of a life based totally on faith.

A discussion about how Unamuno and twentieth-century existential thought fit into the fallibilist tradition is a fascinating topic but will not be considered in this essay; existentialism is mentioned here as a contrast to the Popperian form of fallibilism argued for throughout this book, which attempts to develop a philosophy which is centered on reason rather than on pure faith. Popper's views about reason are one possible way to hold a fallibilistic *rational* perspective toward life. As we have noted, Dewey and Russell also developed fallibilistic ideas which sought to find a significant place for reason. Thus, most twentieth-century philosophers have had to deal with the question, "How can human beings live in a world where they can never know the absolute truth?" This question is the underlying basis of a fallibilistic world view: *both rationalists and irrationalists* have been aware of human fallibility.

The writings in this book belong to the rationalist camp within the fallibilistic tradition. Although, as we have stated, fallibilists who are also rationalists have profoundly different views about,

and theories of, human reason, what often separates rational fallibilists from their irrationalist opponents is that rationalists have
tried to demonstrate that the choice between competing ideas is
not necessarily totally arbitrary or strictly a matter of faith. For
rationalists, the choice between competing ideas, particularly scientific hypotheses, can be affected by appealing to experience and
other forms of arguments which are not entirely subjective. Rationalists such as Russell, Dewey, and Popper have argued that
scientists are not entirely arbitrary when they choose among alternative and competing theories, and rationalists often consider the
scientific enterprise as the model for how human beings can make
decisions. In order to gain an understanding of how contemporary
fallibilists have differed in their views of reason and the scientific
method, let us now turn to some of Russell's notions about science and induction.

In many of his works Russell suggested that in order to view
science as a rational enterprise it is necessary to accept the process
of induction as a way of deciding if some ideas are better than
others. Russell also endorsed Hume's claim that induction cannot
demonstrate that scientific and empirical theories are absolutely
true. Russell at times has even suggested that it is somewhat unreasonable to use inductive procedures. But despite Russell's mis-
givings about induction, he saw no way to preserve reason and
science without the use of induction. Thus, although Russell was
quite aware of the significance of what Hume had written about
justifying ideas by accumulating verifying experiences, he nevertheless found it desirable for science to rely on inductive principles. In answering Hume's criticism of induction, Russell once
wrote:

Hume's scepticism rests entirely upon his rejection of the
principle of induction. . . . If this principle is not true, every
attempt to arrive at general scientific laws from particular
observations is fallacious. . . . Hume has proved that pure
empiricism is not a sufficient basis for science. But if this one
principle [i.e., the principle of induction] is admitted, everything else can proceed in accordance with the theory that all
our knowledge is based on experience. It must be granted

that this is a serious departure from pure empiricism, and
that those who are not empiricists may ask why, if one departure is allowed, others are to be forbidden. These, however,
are questions not directly raised by Hume's arguments. What
these arguments prove—and I do not think the proof can be
controverted—is that induction is an independent logical
principle, incapable of being inferred either from experience
or from other logical principles, and that without this principle science is impossible.[18]

When Russell accepted the principle of induction as a major
aspect of the method of science, he knowingly allowed a degree of
faith and unreasonableness to enter into his philosophy of science.
However, it would be wrong to view Russell as an irrationalist. On
the contrary, many rationalists have realized that there are *limitations* on human reason; and theories of rationality have at times
been viewed as means to diminish the irrational in life. That is,
some rationalists have endorsed the notion that a totally comprehensive rationalistic philosophy is not possible; rather than completely reject reason, some modern rationalists such as Russell
have tried to find a *limited* place for reason in the life of human
beings.

The fallibilistic philosophy developed by Russell parallels
Hume's philosophy in many ways. As was true of Hume, Russell
spent much of his life being torn between believing in induction
and realizing that induction could not demonstrate the absolute
truthfulness of scientific ideas. And following Hume, Russell tried
to answer the question, "How can experience demonstrate and
justify that our ideas, and particularly scientific theories, are absolutely true?" This question, previously labeled *the Humian problem of induction,* deeply interested Russell; given the fact that
induction could not demonstrate the truthfulness of scientific
ideas, he had to acknowledge that science did not stand on firm
ground—its theories could not be shown to be absolutely true.
But, as noted, since Russell could not imagine that science could
function without induction or absolute truth as its aim, he found
it both necessary and desirable to claim the following: (1) that

induction is the method of the empirical sciences; (2) that induction could not demonstrate the absolute truthfulness of scientific theories; and (3) that absolute truth should be the *unattainable* goal of scientific inquiry.

Russell's views on science represent many of the conflicts and dilemmas that twentieth-century human beings have had to live with. That is, moderns must realize that no matter how successful science is, it is *always* possible that someone like Einstein will appear and create ideas that overturn the foundations of current scientific views. Although philosophers such as Dewey and Popper were able to make some adjustments to the Humian way of looking at science and truth, it was Russell's fate not to be able to go beyond what Hume had said.

DEWEY'S VIEWS: REFORMULATION OF THE HUMIAN PROBLEM

Let us now turn to a discussion of Dewey's views on induction and the scientific method. Dewey was born in 1859, and it is often pointed out that this is the year in which Charles Darwin (1809–82) published his famous *Origin of Species*. Darwin's book had a tremendous impact on the way people came to look upon science and scientific knowledge. As is well known, at the heart of Darwin's evolutionary theory is the idea that species evolve and change as time goes on. Eventually, philosophers such as Dewey began to realize not only that species evolved but also that human institutions and human ideas evolved or changed over time. In regard to the influence Darwin's ideas were to have on science and human inquiry, Dewey wrote:

the "Origin of Species" introduced a mode of thinking that in the end was bound to transform the logic of knowledge, and hence the treatment of morals, politics, and religion. . . . the vivid and popular features of the anti-Darwinian row tended to leave the impression that the issue was between science on one side and theology on the other. Such was not the case—

the issue lay primarily within science itself, as Darwin himself early recognized.[19]

Later in his essay on Darwin's evolutionary theory, Dewey stated:

What does our touchstone indicate as to the bearing of Darwinian ideas upon philosophy? In the first place, the new logic outlaws, flanks, dismisses—what you will—one type of problems and substitutes for it another type. Philosophy foreswears inquiry after absolute origins and absolute finalities in order to explore specific values and the specific conditions that generate them.[20]

Dewey wrote these comments about Darwin's ideas in 1909. It is to Dewey's credit that he was one of the first to understand that Darwin's views on evolution would have a great impact, not only on biology but also on the way philosophers would come to view human knowledge. Specifically, Dewey understood that old views about science had to change in light of Darwin's discoveries. He also saw that the changes necessary were basic to the development of a philosophical framework. For Dewey, not only would people have to change the ideas they had about knowledge, but they would also have to *learn how to ask new questions* about science, the growth of knowledge, and human inquiry in general.

Darwinian theories not only influenced Dewey's philosophy but also helped Dewey better explain the pragmatic view of truth. Significantly, once Dewey concluded that the goal of inquiry was no longer absolute truth but pragmatic truth, Dewey was in a position to *reformulate* the Humian problem of induction. The problem of induction could be formulated with a question such as, "How can experience demonstrate and justify that our ideas, and particularly scientific theories, are *pragmatically* true?" This question, which we can refer to as *the Deweyan problem of induction,* is very similar to the question Hume asked with regard to induction. But there is a difference. Dewey's question assumes his answer to the problem of the aim of science; the Deweyan problem of induction incorporates some of his own ideas about scientific knowledge evolving from one truth to another truth. By reformulating the problem of induction, Dewey was able to avoid Hume's criticism that induction could not demonstrate that scientific ideas were absolutely true.

The question labeled the Deweyan problem of induction was not directly asked by Dewey; this question is a historical conjecture about the question Dewey was seeking an answer to when he dealt with issues related to an explanation of the scientific method. If Dewey did reformulate the problem of induction in a way similar to our conjectured question, then the Humian criticism of induction would have been fairly easy for him to ignore. Since Dewey readily admitted that science and its method of inquiry could not justify that scientific theories were absolutely true, he had no problem in agreeing with Hume. However, Dewey did disagree with Hume over the *aim of science*. Furthermore, he believed that induction continued to be an important and helpful tool for determining that some conclusions were more warranted or valid than others. That is, Dewey required that scientific hypotheses be supported by experience; scientific conclusions could not become totally dependent upon the whims or on the arbitrary decisions of scientists. Thus, for Dewey induction was the means by which scientists gained some assurance that their suggested theories were valid in relationship to known experiences. In regard to the use of inductive procedures in science, Dewey once noted the following:

> The problem of inductive inquiry, and the precautions that have to be observed in conducting it, all have to do with ascertaining that the given case *is* representative, or is a sample or specimen. There is no doubt that *some* cases, several or many, have to be examined in the course of inquiry; this is necessarily involved in the function of comparison-contrast within inquiry. But the validity of the inferred conclusion does not depend upon their number. On the contrary, the survey and operational comparison of several cases is strictly instrumental to determination of what actually takes place in *one* case. The moment *one* case is determined to be such that it is an exemplary representative, the problem in hand is solved.[21]

This excerpt is from Dewey's *Logic: The Theory of Inquiry*. In this book, which was published in 1938 as Dewey was approaching his eightieth birthday, one sees the product of a life's work in trying to understand how human beings go about the process of acquiring knowledge. Dewey's *Logic* was published well after Einstein's ideas had shown that even knowledge in physics might change. But Dewey realized that all changes would not necessarily lead to improvement; he knew that some changes would lead to degeneration. Since he wished to demonstrate how the evolution of scientific knowledge did indeed constitute advancement rather than degeneration, Dewey needed to explain how change in science signified an improved understanding of the world. Moreover, Dewey felt a need to explain how a rational enterprise such as science could accept Newton's ideas for such a long period of time. For Dewey, the stability that existed in science for hundreds of years needed to be viewed as rational rather than irrational.

Scientific advance, the stability of science, and the rationality of the scientists were all partially accounted for by Dewey's endorsement of induction as the method of science. Like others before him, Dewey could not imagine that science could function without induction; induction was the method by which scientists helped to advance knowledge by rational means. In other words, for Dewey, scientists accepted or believed their theories because these theories had inductive support and because they were warranted by known experiences. But a new and innovative idea might eventually become even *more* warranted than well-established theories if scientists were able to have new experiences which validated a new idea: when an innovative hypothesis was able to gain the support of new experiences, it could replace an older theory. It is important to remember that Dewey and the other pragmatists were willing to say that science can only know a "truth" relative to known evidence. And for pragmatists, what is viewed as "true" today may not be "true" tomorrow because new experiences may lead to a new "truth." However, as was the case with Russell and Hume, Dewey was not willing to break with traditional Western thought when it came to describing the method of science. Thus, Dewey remained conservative and traditional in deciding that induction was indeed the method of science.

Clearly, Dewey was not especially concerned with Hume's claim that no amount of inductive support could demonstrate that an idea was absolutely true. Dewey could rather easily ignore much of Hume's thinking on induction because he endorsed a pragmatic philosophical perspective which had given up Hume's quest for certainty and absolute truth. For Dewey and the other pragmatists, induction did not perform the function Hume had hoped it would. In Dewey's view, those theories which could not be verified by some experiences should not be accepted by reasonable scientists; and those theories which could be verified by experience should be *tentatively* accepted until scientists developed better ideas. Finally, new and better ideas would have to pass the test of gaining inductive support before they could be accepted as a new scientific "truth."

Dewey's philosophy of science is a highly sophisticated system of ideas which attempted to explain how scientific knowledge evolves over time. As we have seen, Dewey was profoundly affected by both Darwin's and Einstein's ideas. He tried to explain that scientific knowledge was never fixed and unchangeable, and he argued that scientific ideas evolved as new generations grappled with old problems and discovered new problems. Although philosophers such as Russell and Popper have rejected many of Dewey's pragmatic ideas, it should be acknowledged that Dewey's work represents an ingenious attempt to develop a fallibilistic philosophy of science that attempted to explain how twentieth-century scientific knowledge evolved from the science of previous centuries.

The philosophy of science developed by Dewey had a profound effect on Dewey's educational outlook.[22] Dewey's inductivist views helped to form the foundation for his educational philosophy. In many ways his ideas about how children learn from experience were essentially restatements of his notions about how scientists learn from experience. In order to understand how Dewey's views on induction were used in his philosophy of education, one need only read the first chapter in this volume, " 'Learning' by Induction." This essay attempts to explain how many contemporary educators who follow in the pragmatic tradition of Dewey have inherited all the logical problems that Hume raised in relationship to the use of induction.

In many ways, this book is an attempt to develop a fallibilistic philosophy of education that is somewhat *incompatible* with pragmatism. The authors follow in the tradition of the Popperian school, which has tried to develop a *noninductivist* philosophy of science. But before we turn to Popper's notions about science, let us conclude our discussion of Dewey's views by noting that his philosophy of science endorses at least the following three ideas: (1) that induction is the method of the empirical sciences; (2) that induction could not demonstrate the absolute truthfulness of scientific theories; and (3) that pragmatic truth and not absolute truth should be the aim of science. It will be remembered that Russell only endorsed the first two assumptions mentioned here and that he strongly disagreed with Dewey about changing the aim of science from absolute to pragmatic truth.

POPPER'S VIEWS: SCIENCE WITHOUT INDUCTION

The story of twentieth-century fallibilism would not be complete without a discussion of Karl Popper and his noninductivist views. Popper was not willing to join Hume, Dewey, and Russell when it came to the view that inductive procedures are the sine qua non of the scientific method. To the contrary, Popper has argued that the growth of scientific knowledge does not have to depend upon ideas that are verifiable or considered to be warranted by inductive procedures. For Popper, the scientific method is best characterized as a theory of experience which helps people *falsify* scientific ideas: he has argued that the method of science is one of using experience to falsify or refute conjectured theories. Hence, *Popper's falsificationist methodology competes with inductivist or verificationist views of the scientific method.*

Popper's views on the scientific method represent a clear break with traditional Western philosophies over the issue of whether induction is necessary for science. Most philosophers of science before Popper were unable to imagine that science could exist

without induction. As we have seen. Hume and Russell understood that it was unreasonable to claim that induction could demonstrate that scientific ideas were absolutely true, but neither
could eliminate induction from his philosophy of science. Dewey
also relied on induction to some extent, although he was willing to
use inductive procedures, not as a means of demonstrating that
ideas were absolutely true, but as a means of lending support for
accepting some ideas as tentatively valid. However, as noted earlier, Popper was not willing to change the aim of science to pragmatic truth. He did not change science's aim but realized that
induction could be eliminated from science, and he has suggested
that the method of science is one of falsifying or refuting theories
in order to get closer to the unattainable goal of absolute truth. In
regard to the importance of refutations in science, Popper has
stated the following:

> The way in which knowledge progresses, and especially our
> scientific knowledge, is by unjustified (and unjustifiable) an-
> ticipations, by guesses, by tentative solutions to our problems,
> by *conjectures*. These conjectures are *controlled* by criticism;
> that is, by attempted *refutations*, which include severely criti-
> cal tests. They may survive these tests; but they can never be
> positively justified: they can neither be established as cer-
> tainly true nor even as "probable" (in the sense of the proba-
> bility calculus). Criticism of our conjectures is of decisive
> importance: by bringing out our mistakes it makes us under-
> stand the difficulties of the problem which we are trying to
> solve. This is how we become better acquainted with our
> problem, and able to propose more mature solutions: the very
> refutation of a theory—that is, of any serious tentative solu-
> tion to our problem—is always a step forward that takes us
> nearer to the truth.[23]

In order to understand how Popper's *noninductivist* philosophy
of science fits into the fallibilistic tradition, it is important to
realize that Popper, as did Hume, Russell, and Dewey, has endorsed the notion that the absolute truth of scientific ideas could
never be justified by the accumulation of verifying experiences.

Given this fact, Popper, like Dewey, saw that there was a need to reformulate the Humian problem of induction ("How can experience demonstrate and justify that our ideas, and particularly scientific theories, are *absolutely* true?"). But Popper could not accept the Deweyan reformulation of the problem of induction ("How can experience demonstrate and justify that our ideas, and particularly scientific theories, are *pragmatically* true?"), because he agreed with Russell that absolute truth must remain the aim of science. Thus, Popper saw the need to reformulate the problem of induction with a question such as, "How can experience help us discover scientific ideas that are closer to the unattainable goal of absolute truth?" This question, which we can refer to as *the Popperian problem of induction,* is consistent with Popper's answer to the problem of the aim of science. That is, the Popperian formulation of the problem of induction assumes that the aim of science is absolute truth.

Early in this introduction it was pointed out that fallibilists have been very interested in the way people ask questions. Of those who have written much about the importance of how problems are formulated, Dewey and Popper rank very high.[24] Both Dewey and Popper realized that a dialogue was somewhat controlled and structured by the questions people attempted to answer. These two great fallibilist philosophers also understood that the problem of induction could be adequately solved only if the Humian problem of induction were *reformulated.* But since Dewey and Popper made different assumptions about the aim of science, they reformulated the problem of induction with different questions. Thus, the twentieth-century debate about how to view the scientific method is not only about how to solve a problem; central to this debate is the problem of *which questions one should ask.*

The dispute between Dewey and Popper about how to reformulate the problem of induction goes back to a consideration of the best solution to the problem of the aim of science ("What should be the goal of scientific inquiry?"). If one accepts Russell's and Popper's criticisms of pragmatic truth as the aim of science, it becomes necessary to reject the Deweyan problem of induction, since this problem is formulated by a question which assumes that pragmatic truth is the aim of science. Popper could not accept the consequences associated with changing the goal of science from absolute to pragmatic truth, and thus he offered his own formulation of the problem of induction.[25]

Popper's surprising answer to the Popperian problem of induction is that the scientific method does not have anything to do with induction or the accumulation of a number of experiences which justify or verify empirical ideas. Following Hume's criticism of induction, Popper has said:

> Now it is far from obvious, from a logical point of view, that we are justified in inferring universal statements from singular ones, no matter how numerous; for any conclusion drawn in this way may always turn out to be false: no matter now many instances of white swans we may have observed, this does not justify the conclusion that *all* swans are white.[26]

But, unlike Hume, Popper does not think that we should require scientific ideas to be either verifiable or falsifiable. Instead, Popper has argued that universal empirical statements need to be decidable only in *one sense*; science need only

> admit as empirical . . . statements which are decidable in one sense only—unilaterally decidable and, more especially, falsifiable—and which may be tested by systematic attempts to falsify them.[27]

Popper's falsificationist theory of experience was an attempt to create a scientific method that incorporated the notion that no amount of positive evidence could demonstrate that a scientific theory was absolutely true. Since Popper wholeheartedly endorsed Hume's criticism of induction, and since he did not want to give up the goal of absolute truth, Popper had to provide an *alternative* to inductivist views of science. According to Popper's *noninductive* scientific method, there is no need for scientists to accumulate a number of positive experiences to justify scientific theories. What is crucial is that scientists propose theories that are potentially falsifiable by experience. Indeed, Popper would consider the falisification of a scientific theory by *one* experience to be a sign of progress, because by eliminating mistaken theories

scientists may then conjecture new theories which might not be
falsified by the experiences which have falsified an old theory.
Thus, for Popper, the growth of scientific knowledge dependens
on *overthrowing or rejecting false theories*. In this regard, Popper
has written:

> it is not the accumulation of observations which I have in
> mind when I speak of the growth of scientific knowledge, but
> the repeated overthrow of scientific theories and their re-
> placement by better or more satisfactory ones. This, in-
> cidentally, is a procedure which might be found worthy of
> attention even by those who see the most important aspect of
> the growth of scientific knowledge in new experiments and in
> new observations. For our critical examination of our theories
> leads us to attempts to test and to overthrow them; and these
> lead us further to experiments and observations of a kind
> which nobody would ever have dreamt of without the stim-
> ulus and guidance both of our theories and of our criticism of
> them.[28]

Popper has often referred to his falsificationist methodology as
a critical-empirical method because it attempts to weed out mistaken ideas. Also, one of the most interesting things about a falsificationist methodology is that it attempts to base the scientific
method on deductive principles.[29] Specifically, Popper's views on
falsifiability suggest that the testing of scientific theories is dependent upon deductions such as the following:

1. All swans are white. (first premise)
2. I saw a black swan in my backyard today. (second premise)
3. Therefore, there are some non-white swans and the first
   premise above is false if indeed the second premise is true.
   (deductive conclusion)

Contemporary philosophers are still debating whether Popper
has been able to develop a view of the scientific method that
eliminates the need for some inductive principles. For our purposes, it is not necessary to examine the finer points of this philosophy; what is significant in the present context is that Popper's

views of the scientific method help explain how scientific knowledge grows and develops through criticism. Popper's work is post-Einsteinian, and his thinking was necessarily affected by the revolution in physics. Like Dewey, Popper developed *an evolutionary view of the growth of scientific knowledge* that allowed ideas to change over time. But there are many differences between Popper's and Dewey's evolutionary views on scientific knowledge. A major difference is, of course, that contrary to Dewey's theory, Popper's evolutionary theory attempts to account for progress without relying on inductive procedures. Another major difference is that Popper has viewed scientific knowledge as evolving toward the infinite and unattainable goal of absolute truth, whereas, as was discussed earlier, Dewey's view of the growth of knowledge suggested that at each stage in the evolutionary process scientists could claim to have a discovered "truth" relative to the known evidence; he did not claim that scientific efforts were aimed at coming closer to the goal of absolute truth.

It would have been highly interesting to see how Dewey might have dealt with Popper's views on the scientific method. Regrettably, a confrontation between Dewey and Popper never materialized. Popper entered the twentieth-century philosophical scene in 1934 with the publication of the German version of his *The Logic of Scientific Discovery*. This book, which is now generally considered one of the classics of contemporary philosophy of science, was not published in English until 1959. By this time Dewey had died, and his *Logic: A Study of Inquiry* had been around for over twenty years. Both Dewey and Popper published books on the philosophy of science during the mid-1930s, but these books had no influence on each other. By the 1930s Dewey had achieved international stature, and his time was no doubt filled with his own work and the work of friends he had acquired over a lifetime. Thus, it would have been very strange indeed if Dewey had read the first book of the then young unknown Viennese philosopher of science. For his part, Popper did not systematically criticize Dewey's ideas; he has been concerned primarily with those European philosophers who have developed ideas similar to those of the American pragmatists.

Both of these great twentieth-century philosophers belong to the fallibilist tradition, and their ideas do have some similarities.

In order to clarify some of the similarities and differences between Popper's and Dewey's ideas, it is useful to state here that Popper has endorsed at least the following three ideas: (1) that the scientific method centers around falsificationist procedures, not inductive procedures; (2) that induction cannot demonstrate the absolute truthfulness of scientific theories; and (3) that absolute truth should be viewed as an infinite and unattainable goal of scientific inquiry. In regard to these three assumptions, Dewey endorsed only the second one and disagreed with the first and third. As for Russell, he agreed with the second and third assumptions, but he also found the rejection of induction to be unsatisfactory.

COMPETING FORMULATIONS OF CONTEMPORARY FALLIBILISM

There are many problems associated with a noninductivist or falsificationist scientific method, and Popper's work does not solve all of these problems. Popper's writings do give some possible directions which some individuals may wish to follow if they decide that science without induction is possible and desirable. Popper's work may leave much to be desired, but his view that science does not need induction in ingenious and still quite novel.

Popper's place in the history of Western philosophy is not well established. It is quite possible that his noninductivist views will not receive much attention in the future; other contemporary philosophers may be able to demonstrate that induction is still the mainstay of science and the scientific method. But if Popper's noninductive views are taken seriously, and if his ideas do indeed hint at the direction the philosophy of science will take, then science and the scientific method will be viewed quite differently in the future.

Before we begin to discuss some of the possible effects of Popper's ideas on educational theory and practice, let us first summarize what has been said about the *three different forms of fallibilism* that have been developed by Russell, Dewey, and Popper. The accompanying table summarizes what has been said about these philosophers' views on fallibilism.

THREE CONTEMPORARY FORMULATIONS
OF FALLIBILISM

Problems and Assumptions to Be Identified	*RUSSELL*	*DEWEY*	*POPPER*
Formulation of the problem of the aim of science	What should be the goal of scientific inquiry (i.e., the problem of the aim of science)?	Same as Russell	Same as Russell
Aim of science	Unattainable absolute truth	Pragmatic truth	Same as Russell
Question asked about scientific method	How can experience demonstrate and justify that our ideas, and particularly scientific theories, are absolutely true and certain (i.e., the Humian problem of induction)?	How can experience demonstrate and justify that our ideas, and particularly scientific theories, are pragmatically true (i.e., the Deweyan problem of induction)?	How can experience help us discover scientific ideas that are closer to the unattainable goal of absolute truth (i.e., the Popperian problem of induction)?
Views on induction and scientific method	Science needs induction, but induction cannot demonstrate that scientific theories are absolutely true.	Science needs induction, but induction demonstrates only that scientific theories are pragmatically true.	Science does not need induction, and experience can help us find out only which of our scientific theories might be false.

A PREVIEW OF THE BOOK

A thorough history of twentieth-century fallibilism still needs to
be written. But with a beginning understanding of contemporary
fallibilism at hand, let us now consider how the following essays
contribute to the development of a fallibilistic educational perspective that is consistent with many of the ideas developed by
Popper and his followers.

This book has been divided into three parts, and the first chapter in each part introduces some of the problems that appear in
the succeeding essays. Also, although the essays have much in common, each author presents a somewhat different interpretation of
how a Popperian form of fallibilism is relevant to schooling. These
differences aside, all of the essays incorporate many of Popper's
ideas about science, truth, and induction. Following is a brief summary of the contents of the following nine chapters.

The first part begins with Stephenie Edgerton's paper, " 'Learning' by Induction." Here Edgerton centers her attention on the
question, "How are the problems associated with induction relevant for current proposals for social studies curriculum and instruction?" This essay explains how Popper's views on induction
are important for social studies theorists; it also suggests that induction may not be a satisfactory method of teaching students in
social study classes. Edgerton's essay is a criticism of all contemporary educational programs which teach children to use inductive
methods, and her paper challenges those educators who follow in
the pragmatic tradition. The second paper of the first part is
Ronald Swartz's "Mistakes as an Important Part of the Learning
Process." This chapter discusses the question, "How can the study
of mistakes be incorporated into the learning process?" In this
paper Swartz argues that Popper's theory of inquiry suggests that
the study of mistakes can significantly enhance learning and recommends that educators need to be more tolerant of the mistakes
students are likely to make. In the last chapter of this part, Henry
Perkinson's paper, "Against Learning," considers the question,
"How can we develop a nonauthoritarian view of classroom learn-

ing?" Perkinson's answer to this question is that many of Popper's ideas about criticism can help teachers behave in a nonauthoritarian manner; and he offers a comprehensive view of how teachers can use criticism as the basis for teaching academic skills, theoretical information, and moral attitudes toward life. In sum, this essay is an attempt to explain that much of the teaching done in contemporary classrooms is authoritarian and Perkinson argues against viewing learning as a process which imposes predetermined learning activities on students.

Part II comprises chapters which attempt to explain how human beings can undertake activities in the interest of educational reforms. In the first essay, "Liberalism and Imaginative Educational Reforms," Swartz asks the question, "How should the imagination of social theorists be both used and checked in the development and implementation of innovative educational reforms?" This essay attempts to apply to social reform some of Popper's ideas about viewing science as a process of conjectures and refutations. Swartz suggests that a Popperian approach to educational improvement relies on many basic liberal assumptions, and he explains why it is desirable to encourage social reformers to be as imaginative as possible. Swartz also recommends that it is desirable to be critical of both conventional and innovative educational theories, and he suggests that at times imaginative educational ideas may be undesirable and too dangerous to use with children. The next chapter in this part is Perkinson's essay, "How to Improve Your School," which treats the question, "What might happen if educators took the notion of human fallibility seriously?" Perkinson argues that a fallibilistic view of educational reform would begin by taking into account the environment in which schooling presently takes place. He develops an ecological approach to social change which suggests that people can start to improve schooling by modifying existing educational institutions. Perkinson's ecological approach to reform uses many of Popper's ideas about criticism and the elimination of error as the basis for educational improvement. Specifically, he argues that we can improve education by trying to eliminate the adverse consequences fostered in contemporary schools. In the last paper in this part, "Skepticism and Schooling," Edgerton discusses the question, "Should the schools be rooted *primarily* in various forms of faith?" She suggests that curriculum development, a crucial aspect of educational reform, has become stagnant because most educators begin by asking questions which assume that it is reasonable to have faith in the idea that professional educators are reliable authorities who possess valuable knowledge that should be taught to all students. Edgerton points out that educators have wrongly assumed that their knowledge claims can be rationally justified and then she explains some of the dangers inherent in schools rooted in the faith that contemporary knowledge is indeed justified by rational means. Also, Edgerton follows Popper in arguing for a critical form of rationality which would require educational reformers to change the kinds of questions which are being asked about curriculum development.

Part III explains how Popper's form of fallibilism might eventually lead to specific kinds of educational innovations. This part begins with Perkinson's essay, "Education and the New Pluralism," in which he asks the question, "What role can education play in a pluralistic society such as the United States?" Perkinson points out that American society has become increasingly pluralistic, and he argues that schools in a pluralistic community can help people learn how to protect themselves from potential dangers. Perkinson suggests that schools can no longer be viewed as social agencies which perform the traditional task of socializing children; he recommends that instead, all those who are affected by the educational process should have the opportunity to use schooling as a means of learning self-protection. The second paper in this final part is Edgerton's "Induction, Skepticism, and Refutation: Learning through Criticism." In this paper Edgerton attempts to answer the question, "How can teachers help students to be critical of the information one is exposed to in the classroom?" This essay focuses on many of the difficulties that arise when teachers try to have children learn ideas through the process of induction. Edgerton points out that students come to all learning situations with many preconceived ideas. Furthermore, she argues that teachers' efforts often fail, since inductive theories of learning ignore the fact that children are in a sense theoreticians who are likely to make diverse interpretations of information. She suggests that teachers need to realize that the ideas presented in the school curriculum can have various interpretations, and she argues that students should be given assistance in learning how to be critical experimentalists who attempt to gain a better understanding of the world. The last chapter in this book is Swartz's "Authority, Responsibility, and Democratic Schooling." In this paper Swartz discusses the question, "How might authority be viewed and used in democratic and nondemocratic schools?" and he attempts to demonstrate that a fallibilistic view of all educational authorities is compatible with the idea of democratic schools. Swartz argues that democratic schooling would require many changes in conventional ideas about how educational programs should service society. It is specifically suggested that in democratic schools students would become fallible authorities who would be allowed to be personally responsible for much of what is learned in school. Moreover, Swartz points out that a fallibilistic view of educational authorities might significantly alter traditional ideas about how students and teachers should interact with one another, and he suggests that the many changes associated with democratic schooling should be tried in experimental educational programs, referred to as self-governing schools. He claims that self-governing educational alternatives are viable learning situations which are educational innovations that rely on a fallibilistic educational perspective.

CONCLUDING REMARKS

I would like to emphasize here that this volume in no way represents a finished educational philosophy that can be readily imposed on our existing educational institutions. In many ways, the essays presented in this book only hint at some possible directions people might wish to explore if they want to improve our schools. As we have noted many times, although disagreements among fallibilists have not been discussed in this introduction, the proponents of a Popperian fallibilistic world view do at times disagree; and this fact shows that there is much room for debate within the fallibilist tradition—and, as is noted in many of the essays, fallibilists welcome and even seek criticism—from fallibilists and nonfallibilists alike. Nevertheless, the authors of this book agree that contemporary educational thinking has, in general, not caught up with the view that our knowledge is more changing and that it is more fallible than pragmatism has suggested. When our educational institutions do come to grips with recent develop- ments within the fallibilist tradition, there will undoubtedly be some major changes in our schools.

NOTES

1. For statements which seem to demonstrate that Russell, Dewey, and Pop- per are all part of the fallibilistic tradition, see the epigraph at the beginning of this introduction. The references for these quotations can be found in the follow- ing works: Bertrand Russell, *Portraits from Memory* (New York: Simon and Schuster, 1967), p. 180; John Dewey, "Progressive Education and the Science of Education," *Dewey on Education*, ed. Martin S. Dworkin (New York: Teachers College Press, 1965), p. 116; Karl R. Popper, *The Open Society and Its Enemies*, vol. 2 (New York: Harper and Row, 1963), p. 375. At this time I would like to thank Susan Swartz, Stephenie Edgerton and Henry Perkinson for the helpful comments they made on a previous draft of this paper. Although I must accept the responsibility for the arguments offered in this introduction, I am very grate- ful for the time that the above mentioned individuals have given to my earlier ideas about the development of a fallibilistic educational philosophy.

2. Leopold Infeld, *Albert Einstein: His Work and Its Influence on Our World* (New York: Charles Scribner's Sons, 1950), p. 10. It should be noted that the words "developed by Newton" in brackets have been added to make Infeld's meaning somewhat clearer.

3. Karl R. Popper, "Intellectual Autobiography," *The Philosophy of Karl Popper*, ed. Paul Arthur Schilpp (LaSalle, Ill.: Open Court, 1974), pp. 19-20.

4. John Dewey, *The Influence of Darwin on Philosophy* (Bloomington, Ind.: Indiana University Press, 1965), p. 19.

5. See Author's Dedication in William James, *Pragmatism and Other Essays* (New York: Washington Square Press, 1968).

6. John Stuart Mill, *On Liberty* (New York: Appleton-Century-Crofts, 1947), p. 21.

7. See Infeld, *Albert Einstein*.

8. Refer to note 15.

9. Charles Sanders Peirce, "The Scientific Attitude and Fallibilism," *Philo- sophical Writings of Peirce*, ed. Justus Buchler (New York: Dover Publications, 1955), p. 58.

10. John Dewey, *The Quest for Certainty: A Study of the Relationship of Knowledge and Action* (New York: G. P. Putman's Sons, 1960), p. 146.

11. John Dewey, *Experience and Education* (New York: Macmillan, 1970), p. 88.

12. John Dewey, *Logic: The Study of Inquiry* (New York: Holt, Rinehart and Winston, 1966), p. 345.

13. Bertrand Russell, *A History of Western Philosophy* (New York: Simon and Schuster, 1945), pp. 827-28.

14. Karl R. Popper, *Conjectures and Refutations: The Growth of Scientific Knowledge* (New York: Basic Books, 1962), pp. 229-30.

15. David Hume, "A Treatise Concerning Human Nature," *British Empirical Philosophers*, ed. A. J. Ayer and Raymond Winch (New York: Simon and Schuster, 1968), p. 412.

16. See Infeld, *Albert Einstein*.

17. Miguel de Unamuno, *Tragic Sense of Life* (New York: Dover Publications, 1954), p. 104.

18. Russell, *A History of Western Philosophy*, pp. 673-74. It should be noted that the words "the principle of induction" which appear in brackets have been added in order to make Russell's meaning somewhat clearer.

19. Dewey, *The Influence of Darwin*, p. 2.

20. Ibid., p. 13.

21. Dewey, *Logic: The Study of Inquiry*, pp. 436-37.

22. Dewey, *Experience and Education*.

23. Popper, *Conjectures and Refutations*, p. vii.

24. See the references in notes 3, 4, 14, 18, and 23.

25. For Popper's account of how he viewed the problem of induction see Karl R. Popper, *Objective Knowledge: An Evolutionary Approach* (London: Oxford University Press, 1974), pp. 1-31.

26. Karl R. Popper, *The Logic of Scientific Discovery* (New York: Harper and Row, 1960), p. 27.

27. Ibid., p. 42.

28. Popper, *Conjectures and Refutations*, pp. 215-16.

29. See Popper, *The Logic of Scientific Discovery*, pp. 32-34 and 40-42.

PART I

On Learning

CHAPTER 1

"Learning" by Induction*

STEPHENIE G. EDGERTON

INTRODUCTION

The eighteenth-century philosopher David Hume insisted that men committed a crucial error when they claimed to justify generalizations by enumerating evidence for them. Hume's argument pointed to the logical mistake of inferring theoretical knowledge from observations. No matter how many swans we may examine and find white, the claim that "All swans are white" may be false. Methods of generalizing from experience have traditionally been labeled "inductive."

Although there is widespread recognition in philosophic circles of the logical problem of induction, to date social studies workers appear undisturbed by this dilemma of empiricism. This is the case even though the most fashionable prescriptions for social studies curriculum and instruction renovation call for "inductive procedures." The relevance of the logical puzzle posed by Hume

* This paper previously appeared in *Social Education* (May 1967), pp. 373–76. The paper presented here contains a few minor changes from the original version. Reprinted with permission of the National Council for the Social Studies.

to current developments in the social studies is the focal point of this paper.

THE INDUCTIVE TRADITION

Since the time of Francis Bacon, men have been enamored of the notion that we accumulate knowledge from experience by using the inductive method.[1]

Suspicious of speculative procedures presumed to be tinged with subjectivity, information gatherers have pursued empirically based rules for the generation of knowledge. Experience (in more technical terms, data) has been considered the only solid footing on which to build theory. Early inductivists envisaged theoretical knowledge emerging lockstep from their observations. They viewed the inductive approach as a guarantee against subjectivity. The removal of armchair speculation from the scientific situation, coupled with empirical finesse, gave comfort to the inquirer fearful of human bias. The Baconian doctrine that prejudice may be overcome by observation was accepted in a very naive form and fostered faith in a formula for the *discovery* of theoretical knowledge.[2]

The modern sophicated inductivist seldom supports a magic formula approach to discovery; he opts, instead, for a formula which *justifies* theoretical knowledge. Such a theorist emphasizes the accumulation of positive cases in warranting generalizations—the procedure commonly known as verification. Although some contemporary inductivists are aware of the nondemonstrative element involved in their approach to the accumulation of theoretical knowledge and rely on a probability calculus, a type of calculation which functions as a confidence raiser, they, like their predecessors, are not immune to the criticisms of David Hume.[3]

THE ARGUMENT OF DAVID HUME

Researchers, inductivists and others, in their quest for theoretical knowledge have always sought broad generalizations, recognizing the potential for explanation and prediction in propositions having a wide scope. Theories which are empirically rich explain a wide variety of phenomena. The highly prized theory is a set of generalizations which encompass, not only observed, but unobserved instances of the matter under investigation. These *unobserved* instances were the source of David Hume's concern.

In his *Treatise of Human Nature* Hume argued that men could not justify their claims regarding phenomena they had not observed.[4] He pointed out that the validity of a generalization which covered unobserved cases could not be demonstrated. Rational assurance that unobserved instances were similar to observed instances was missing and appeared impossible of attainment. The "inductive leap" from a singular statement (or set of statements) to a universal statement was logically impermissible. No guarantee could be given that the future would resemble the past; no certification was available that though two elements of a situation had been related, they would be so related in cases as yet unobserved.

Hume indicated that the consequences of appealing to experience in order to justify conclusions regarding unobserved instances involved an infinite regress. Put simply, in order to justify generalizations covering unobserved instances, what is needed is a principle of inference which permits the transition from observed to unobserved cases. But such a principle, necessarily universal, creates the same difficulty which occasioned its introduction. To justify this principle, a higher-order principle must be introduced. An infinite regress has been generated.[5]

Philosophers have attempted to resolve the problem of induction for over one hundred years. No acceptable solution has been offered, leaving inductive procedures without rational justification, that is, grounded on faith.

THE NEED FOR CLARIFICATION

Considering the problem of induction, might it not be appropriate to ask educators interested in the social studies whether they have inherited a thorny difficulty in prescribing an inductive approach to teachers? Do currently proposed instructional tech-

niques lack a rational defense? Before answers may be attempted
to these questions, it seems desirable to inquire into the present
designs for reform in the social studies.

Clearly, "the new social studies" favors an emphasis on methods
of inquiry. This emphasis becomes obvious upon examination of
recently published textbooks for prospective social studies teachers. The titles of these texts alone are indicative of the new look.
For example, there are: Clements, Fielder, and Tabachnick's *Social Study: Inquiry in Elementary Classrooms*, Massialas and
Cox's *Inquiry in Social Studies*, and Fenton's *Teaching the New
Social Studies in Secondary Schools: An Inductive Approach*.
However, although inquiry is the fashionable approach, it is in no
way self-evident that inductive procedures of inquiry, in the traditional sense, are being proposed. The term "inductive" is attached
to a variety of activities, some of which do not appear to be inductive in the strictest sense.

Moreover, some procedures which are inductive are not so labeled. For instance, it is not obvious that the modern followers of
John Dewey's philosophy of instruction prescribe inductive procedures. Of course, they do when they urge that children be
taught to verify propositions. Hunt and Metcalf insist that "No
conclusion is regarded as final until it has been verified against
data from nature" while at the same time indicating that "The
aim of testing is to provide support, rather than conclusive verification, for a hypothesis." [6] A similar position is taken by Massialas and Cox in their discussion of the reflective model.[7]

Interestingly, at first glance the advocates of the "inductive approach," "discovery teaching," "discovery inquiry," and "inductive
discovery" appear open to the charge of advocating a logically
unjustifiable method of inquiry, whereas closer inspection suggests
that the problem of induction may be more directly relevant to
the proponents of "reflective" or "problem-solving" method.[8]
Why is this?

Typically, discussions of the inductive approach and the like
lack clarity. Current social studies theorists do not indicate in
their suggested prescriptions for curriculum design and teaching
practices whether they mean to imply under the label of induction
that:

1. "Children learn inductively"; or
2. "Inductive procedures of inquiry are a valid method for accumulating knowledge"; or
3. Both or neither.

Obviously, claims 1 and 2 are different claims. Claim 1 is an empirical assertion purporting to describe human behavior. To assert claim 1 is to claim that *as a matter of fact* children learn inductively; and, perhaps, to suggest that children learn more efficiently or creatively when learning inductively. Presumably such a claim could be accompanied by a stipulation of the conditions under which it obtained; for example, age. On the other hand, to assert claim 2 is to claim that inductive procedures are logically admissible. The procedures in question are generalizing from data and, its reverse, verification.

Admittedly, a social studies theorist seldom is asked to justify his classroom prescriptions. However, were he asked, his arguments would reflect the meaning he attached to the notion of induction. If his prescriptions were based on claim 1, or variations thereof, then, appropriately, he would justify his proposals by giving arguments grounded in psychological theory. No doubt, inductive learning theory would emerge as a competitor of other learning theories.[9] If, however, his prescriptions were based on claim 2, he would advance arguments for the validity of inductive methods of research. The problem of induction would face him immediately.

While a theorist who labels his approach "inductive" may avoid the problem of induction, the neo-Deweyite could be harassed in either of two contexts. The difficulty is least likely to arise in the context of discovery. Rarely do contemporary advocates of the method of inquiry suggest in a bald manner that generalizations spring from a collection of pure data. Emphasizing the reflective process, hypotheses are available from diverse sources, numbering among them encounters with similar problems and another person's notion. Rigid empiricism does not seem to mark this genre of theorists. Telling, however, is the insistence that verification be a major step in the problem-solving process. Like it or not, verification is reverse induction. That is, in the context of justification,

warranting a generalization involves the inductive leap. Whereas
refutation necessitates only one negative case, verification demands the counting of every case. Unless we refer to a closed class,
verification is, in principle, impossible. Few people recognize that
the process of verification is induction in the reverse. It is the
philosopher of science, Sir Karl R. Popper, who has reminded us
repeatedly of this difficulty.[10]

Confronted with the problem of induction, social studies theorists may appeal to the theory of probability. Following the approach of many social science researchers, it may be argued that
although one cannot "legitimately" generalize or teach students
to generalize, a calculus of probability may be used and "truth"
estimated. This, of course, is to suggest that patterns or trends
may be calculated which may or may not apply to individual cases.
But it is the individual case in which we are interested.

Even probability calculus does not avoid the difficulty surround-
ing the problem of induction, for a principle of probable inference
is necessary to warrant this type of reasoning—a principle the in-
voking of which leads once again to an infinite regress.[11]

A METHODOLOGICAL MISTAKE

To the critic who poses the Humian puzzle, the educator may
respond that verification procedures to date are the best indicator
for estimating the validity of factual propositions. Therefore the
problem of induction is somewhat academic, since we must make
decisions and we must teach children to make decisions, prefer-
ably rational ones.

Does this argument point to a potential confusion? Further,
does it suggest an algorismic emphasis which oversimplifies highly
problematic aspects of social studies curriculum and instruction?

Traditionally, educators interested in the social studies have
taken as an overarching goal "preparation for citizenship." [12] The
emphasis in the new social studies on the *process* instead of the
product seems to imply that a formula may be taught children
which will assist them in being better citizens as well as prudent
individuals. Since the process being proposed is a formula which
aims at warranting descriptive propositions, the maximum out-

come, ideally, of implementation would appear to be an informed population. Substituting the method of the researcher for his product appears unnecessary unless an assumption is being made that the method of the scholar is appropriate for decision making, both personal and public. Is not the researcher in a position superior to that of children (for that matter, of teachers) to concern himself with the warrant for particular propositions and to indicate the level of confidence we may place in his description, theoretical or otherwise? Have social studies educators confused a method of inquiry seemingly appropriate for the validation of knowledge claims with a method appropriate for policymaking? [13]

Following the rationale of many social studies theorists, it would appear that at least two methodologies are necessary to achieve good citizenship: a method of validating propositions and a method for decision making. Or are there three? We may teach children game or decision theory as developed by mathematicians, logicians, and economists. Children would then be in possession of a formula by which they might arrive at the strategies for achieving stipulated ends. But now they must be taught a formula for deciding upon the ends. Somewhere in the scholars' universe there must be a formula for making value judgments. Of course, there is: we may calculate anything. The question is: How good is our calculation?

I, personally, cannot endorse the quest for formulas.[14] I think an adequate explanation of this quest may be found in the spirit of inductivism. Pragmatists may argue that they long ago rejected the quest for certainty and, therefore, that they operate in a non-inductivist climate. But social studies literature indicates that this is not the case. The quest for *certain* formulas has been replaced on the part of the pragmatist, if at all, merely by a quest for *successful* formulas. Pragmatists might profitably consider the demarcation between prophecy and prediction.

CONCLUSION

This discussion began by seeking the relevance of the logical problem of induction to current proposals for social studies curriculum and instruction. Since the proposals lack clarity, it is difficult to assess the relevance. Viewed as imitators of selected methodological facets of their scientific parents, the new social studies may expect to inherit the contentious as well as prestigious features of their models. If social studies curriculum and instruction proposals continue in the direction of their present emphasis, the problem of induction is likely to form part of their inheritance. However, the methodology of applied science and technology may prove to be a rabbit in the hat of social studies educators, for inductive procedures in some respects appear to be appropriate to this family of activities.

NOTES

1. This point of view is taken by the National Council for the Social Studies in the policy statement, *A Guide to Content in the Social Studies*, Report of the NCSS Committees on Concepts and Values. (Washington, D.C.: The Council, 1957, p. 31.) The committees' report:

> "11. The scholars of classical antiquity made many improvements in human living but their method was deductive: a reasoning from the general to the particular. The technique of experimentation was not among their tools.

> "12. The development of inductive reasoning: from the particular to the general, was the step which separated the ancient world from the modern. The sciences which are the basis of today's living began with inductive reasoning. Generally attributed to Francis Bacon, it has substituted mechanical energy for muscle power and has extended our world down into the atom and outward to the stars.

> "13. Recorded history provides many specific examples of how man's life has been made richer and more comfortable through the application of intelligence, and especially the experimental production. For examples: the steam engine, Eli Whitney's ideas of interchangeable parts and mass production, the electric dynamo, the many applications of electricity to the operation of machines, the rotary printing press, etc."

Counterexamples to the notion that modern science began with, or is based on, inductive reasoning are the achievements of Galileo and Einstein. However, the implication that technology is based on inductive reasoning may be accurate.

2. An interesting discussion of the discovery aspects of scientific activity is Norwood Russell Hanson's paper, "Is There a Logic of Scientific Discovery?" *Australasian Journal of Philosophy* 38: (August 1960): 91–106. Hanson thinks there is a logical pattern in the discovery of theories, but not the formula of the naive inductivist. For provocative comments on psychological aspects of scientific research, see T. Kuhn, "The Essential Tension: Tradition and Innovation in

Scientific Research," *Research Conference on the Identification of Creative Scientific Talent*, ed. Calvin W. Taylor (Utah, 1959), pp. 162–77. "But both my own experience in scientific research and my reading of the history of sciences lead me to wonder whether flexibility and open-mindedness have not been too exclusively emphasized as the characteristics requisite for basic research. I shall therefore suggest below that something like 'convergent thinking' is just as essential to scientific advance as is divergent."

3. No attempt is made in this paper to articulate the psychological account of our beliefs given by Hume.

4. David Hume, *A Treatise of Human Nature*, ed. L. A. Selby-Bigge, first edition (Oxford, 1888).

5. It is important to note that Hume's arguments apply to the so-called hypothetico-deductive inference as well as induction by enumeration. An interesting discussion of this may be found in Wesley C. Salmon, "The Foundations of Scientific Inference," *Mind and Cosmos, Essays in Contemporary Science and Philosophy*, ed. Robert G. Colodny (Pittsburgh: University of Pittsburgh Press, 1966), pp. 135–275.

6. See Maurice P. Hunt and Lawrence E. Metcalf, *Teaching High School Social Studies: Problems in Reflective Thinking and Social Understanding* (New York: Harper, 1955), pp. 50–88. The authors disclose their inductivist tendencies in their discussion of verification as well as in their reasons for rejecting intuition as a source of knowledge.

7. Byron G. Massialas and C. Benjamin Cox, *Inquiry in Social Studies* (New York: McGraw-Hill, 1966); Byron G. Massialas, "Teaching History as Inquiry," *New Perspectives in World History*, ed. Shirley H. Engle, Thirty-fourth Yearbook (Washington, D.C.: The National Council for the Social Studies, 1964), pp. 625–59, Byron G. Massialas, ed., "The Indiana Experiments in Inquiry: Social Studies." *Bulletin of the School of Education* 39: [Indiana University] (May 1963): 1–139. It should be noted that, in contrast to Hunt and Metcalf, the Indiana inquiry group appears to foster intuition as a source of hypotheses.

8. I include in this genre the works of, among others, Edwin Fenton, *Teaching the New Social Studies in Secondary Schools: An Inductive Approach* (New York: Holt, Rinehart and Winston, 1966); Hilda Taba, Samuel Levine, and Freeman F. Elzey, *Thinking in Elementary School Children* (San Francisco: San Francisco State College, 1964); U.S. Office of Education Cooperative Research Project 1574; many Project Social Studies staffs, as reported in *Social Education* 30 (April 1965): 206n.

9. This, of course, is merely to shift the focus of the problem of induction to the psychologist, who must then justify his position, in particular, the status of his claims and his methodology.

10. Karl R. Popper, *The Logic of Scientific Discovery* (New York: Basic Books, 1959), and *Conjectures and Refutations: The Growth of Scientific Knowledge* (New York: Basic Books, 1962).

11. For an introductory account of probability calculus, see Ernest Nagel,

"Principles of the Theory of Probability," *Foundations of the Unity of Science*, [*International Encyclopedia of Unified Science*], vol. 1, no. 6 (Chicago: University of Chicago Press, 1939), pp. 1-80. For a discussion of the problem of induction which takes up theories of probability see Popper, *The Logic of Scientific Discovery*.

12. Unlike Cinderella, citizenship is not neglected in the new social studies, e.g., "What about civic education? Preparation for citizenship is implied in each of the three groups of objectives listed above: a set of attitudes and values in keeping with a democratic credo, the ability to use the mode of inquiry, and knowledge of content . . . that provides information about institutional settings and other data essential to a rational decision-making process. But this threefold way of looking at objectives casts civics education in a new light." Fenton, *Teaching the New Social Studies*, p. vii.

Those who opt for "creative" citizenship through the inductive approach might consider Thomas Kuhn's comment: "The troublesome distinctions between basic research, applied research, and invention, need far more research. Nevertheless, it seems likely, for example, that the applied scientist, to whose problems no scientific paradigm need be fully relevant, may profit by a far broader and less rigid education than that to which the pure scientist has characteristically been exposed. Certainly there are many episodes in the history of technology in which lack of more than the most rudimentary scientific education has proved to be an immense help. This group scarcely needs to be reminded that Edison's electric light was produced in the face of unanimous scientific opinion that the arc light could not be 'subdivided,' and there are many other episodes of the sort. . . . If I read the working papers correctly, they suggest that most of you are really in search of the *inventive* personality, a sort of person who does emphasize divergent thinking but whom the United States has already produced in abundance. In the process you may be ignoring certain essential requisites of the basic scientist, a rather different sort of person to whose ranks America's contributions have as yet been notoriously weak. Since most of you are, in fact, Americans, this correlation may not be entirely coincidental." Kuhn, "The Essential Tension," pp. 173-74.

13. It should be noted that the work of Donald W. Oliver and James P. Shaver, *Teaching Public Issues in the High School* (Boston: Houghton Mifflin, 1966), is a special case and is not open to this criticism. These authors question the relevance of the structural frameworks utilized by scholars in the various disciplines as well as their modes of thought to social studies objectives (pp. 230-231). Their jurisprudential approach necessitates comment beyond the scope of this discussion.

14. The recent dialogue of C. Benjamin Cox, "An Inquiry into Inquiries," *Social Education* 29 [May 1965]: 300-302; Malcolm Collier, "A Question about Questions" *(Social Education* 29 *[December 1965]*: 555-56; Herbert M. Kliebard, "In Search of Modes of Inquiry" *(Social Education* 30 [December 1965]:556-558, seems indicative of the "quest" climate among many social studies educators.

CHAPTER 2

Mistakes As an Important Part of the Learning Process*

RONALD M. SWARTZ

INTRODUCTION

In this essay I discuss the question, "How can the study of mistakes be incorporated into the learning process?" I will refer to this question as *the problem of studying mistakes*. My aim is to contribute to the development of a philosophy of education that views mistakes as an integral part of learning.[1]

Before beginning to discuss the problem of studying mistakes, I wish to point out that this essay is not merely an attempt to provide a solution to a problem. I work out of an intellectual tradition that encourages people to understand and explain their problem situation before they discuss solutions to a problem.[2] Unfortunately, people are often in such a rush to solve a problem that they do not take time to explain the sense in which they view their problems. I have here decided to take a leisurely approach to

* This paper previously appeared in the *High School Journal* Volume 59, Number 6, (March 1976), pp. 246-57. Copyright © The University of North Carolina Press. Reprinted by permission of the publisher. The paper presented here contains a few minor changes from the original version.

13

problem solving because I believe it is important for educators to understand the problem of studying mistakes before they discuss and possibly use solutions to this problem.

OVERVIEW OF THE ARGUMENT

The notion that mistakes are an important part of learning is not a new idea. Such philosophers as John Stuart Mill, Bertrand Russell, John Dewey, and Karl Popper have pointed out that mistakes are often an inevitable aspect of human activity and inquiry. These philosophers, and others like them, have suggested that all human knowledge is potentially fallible and mistaken; my plan here is to partly explain how the study of mistakes can become part of an educational program.[3] Although I will deal with many theoretical ideas about mistakes and the learning process, my aim is as much practical as theoretical; I would like to suggest that it is desirable to develop educational policies that view mistakes in a positive way.

I will argue that mistakes can be incorporated into a school's curriculum by exposing children to the notion that problem solving is a dynamic phenomenon. I will suggest that contemporary knowledge can be changed and improved, since we can always find more satisfactory solutions to the problems that interest us. Furthermore, I make the claim that the ephemeral nature of human knowledge can be demonstrated through the study of both the past and present solutions to problems: problems can be studied historically. People should be exposed both to the best and latest solutions to problems and also to those solutions that are presently viewed as mistaken.

The problem of studying mistakes interests me because of its potential effects on an educational program. Unfortunately, many contemporary educational programs are far from viewing mistakes in a positive light; teachers and students often view mistakes as things which should be avoided or concealed. Although some contemporary educators have implied that mistakes are an important part of learning, most contemporary educational programs have not developed systematic policies about how to make mistakes an important part of the process of inquiry.[4]

My discussion of the problem of studying mistakes provides a partial answer to the question, "How can we help people learn once they have chosen a problem to study?" This larger educational question is immense; my interest here is only with a small aspect of it. However, I am not providing a partial answer to the question, "What are the most worthy problems and ideas for children to study and learn while they are in school?" This perennial educational problem is not one that interests me, since I belong to that small group of educators who think that children should be personally responsible for determining their own curriculum.[5]

The problem of studying mistakes is of great interest to me also because I think it is desirable to create a teaching and learning theory that will help people learn how to develop interests and solve problems. I have no desire to tell people what they should study, but I do wish to help people find ways to develop and expand their interests. It is my hope that taking a positive attitude toward mistakes will help children and teachers see that interests can be developed even though people often make errors. In short, mistakes do not have to be obstacles to progress; instead, they can be used as a positive force for improvement.

FIVE ASSUMPTIONS ABOUT MISTAKES AND LEARNING

When people ask the question, "How can the study of mistakes be incorporated into the learning process?" they usually have made a number of assumptions about mistakes and learning. It is an interesting and important point that all questions make a number of both implicit and somewhat explicit assumptions.[6] Questions are not asked out of the clear blue. I would now like to articulate five assumptions that will help explain the way in which I view the problem of studying mistakes.

First, for a number of people it is undisputable that mistakes are an inevitable and unavoidable part of any human activity.[7] No matter how hard people may try to be perfect, they usually make mistakes. Even if perfection were attained, human beings could not know if they were perfect, since there is no possible method or authority that can guarantee that any of our decisions or actions are indeed perfect.[8] All authorities and methods can be viewed as potentially fallible, and human beings must learn to live with the notion that all their decisions and actions are *potentially* mistaken.

Second, since mistakes can be viewed as an inevitable part of life, it seems reasonable to try to find something good about the mistakes people are likely to make; we can try to be optimistic about our mistakes.[9] Of course we all realize that some mistakes are painful or very unpleasant, and some of us may even wish that people would not have to make mistakes. Be that as it may, it is possible to view mistakes as part of the human quest for improving ideas and actions.

Third, the discovery and elimination of mistakes can be seen as one way to improve and to get closer to the goals of truth and perfection.[10] The identification of a mistake helps us get closer to the truth because it enables us to know what we should not do. Such information can free us from our traditional ideas and actions and has the potential of allowing us to consider new ways of doing things. When we are aware of our old mistakes, we are encouraged to rethink our problems and the issues that confront us. This rethinking process may allow us to improve and get closer to truth and perfection.

Fourth, it is possible to view truth and perfection as unattainable goals which are both worthy and desirable to strive for.[11] Although one can readily admit that people may never achieve perfection or reach the truth, philosophers such as Karl Popper and Bertrand Russell have written extensively on the desirability and reasonableness of striving for these unattainable goals. Their arguments about the quest for unattainable goals can be summarized briefly. Unattainable goals are desirable to strive for because they provide a kind of built-in mechanism for seeking improvement. The notion of seeking unattainable goals has not been endorsed because people wish to frustrate individuals; the search for unattainable goals is viewed as desirable because of its potential for encouraging human beings to constantly improve themselves and their ideas.

Fifth, it is possible to make decisions and act in the world in spite of the fact that we might admit that all of our decisions and actions may prove to be mistaken. For a person who thinks that all knowledge is fallible, decisions and actions can be viewed as tests or experiments which may lead to the discovery of a mistake.[12] And, as we will see later in this paper, as long as people can control the harm done by their mistakes, they may be able to use these mistakes as an important part of the quest for improvement. It is extremely important, however, to understand that some kinds of mistakes may have serious damaging consequences for ourselves and others. Thus, one must be careful about the risks one is willing to take in the interest of improvement—a willingness to accept mistakes as inevitable and as constructive should not be equated with irresponsible risk taking.

The foregoing assumptions can be summarized as follows: (1) mistakes can be seen as an unavoidable and inevitable part of any human activity; (2) it is possible to be optimistic about mistakes, because mistakes can be used to help people improve; (3) the discovery and elimination of mistakes can be seen as one way to get closer to the goals of truth and perfection; (4) it is possible to decide to search for unattainable goals such as truth and perfection; and (5) people can make decisions, and act in the world, in spite of the fact that they are uncertain about whether their decisions or actions are true or perfect.

My discussion of these five points should not be taken as a comprehensive statement about all the issues I associate with the study of mistakes. Nevertheless, with this introduction in hand, we are now better able to see how the study of mistakes might fit into an educational program. For the remainder of this paper, I plan to offer a solution to the problem of studying mistakes that is consistent with the five assumptions stated here.

MISTAKES AND PROBLEM SOLVING

If the study of mistakes is to be incorporated into an educational program, one of the first things we must do is try to be clear about the problem or question a theory, decision, or action is related to.[13] Mistakes can be seen as suggested solutions to particular problem situations; if we do not know the context of a mistake, we will be unable to understand how it is relevant to our life and world.

The importance of relating a mistake to a problem situation cannot be overstated. This point is crucial because we can understand if a decision or action is mistaken only if it is related to some context. For example, the notion that it is a mistake to kill people should be judged only in relationship to problems such as, "Should we kill people who have been convicted of murder?" and "Should we kill people who are threatening our lives with a gun?" These are different problems, and a person may decide that it is correct to kill people in none, one, or both of these situations.

The notion of relating decisions and actions to a problem does not necessarily suggest that mistakes are relative to a person's particular point of view or personal preference. This notion suggests that judgments about mistakes are relative to specific problem situations. Within all problem situations people can assume that any solution is potentially either true or false: the notion that mistakes are made within the context of a problem situation does not have to be associated with some relative or subjective view of truth and falsity.

A final point in this regard is that being specific about problem situations allows people to have a way to judge and work for improvement. If we discover that a solution to a problem is mistaken, hopefully we can improve our ideas and actions by discovering new and better solutions.

MISTAKES AND SPECIFIC PROBLEM SITUATIONS

My second point about how to make mistakes an important part of the learning process is that we should try, whenever possible, to carefully consider what kinds of mistakes we might be willing to make in specific problem areas. Put simply, the mistakes we might make in some problem areas are not as serious as those that we might make in others.[14] For example, consider the case of students who are studying the problem, "What is the shape of the planet earth?" Children studying this problem do not do themselves physical harm if they suggest that the earth is like a thin pancake floating in space. On the other hand, students interested in the problem of whether they can stop a bullet with their hand could do themselves serious harm if they experimented to find out.

The mistakes we make may have unforeseen or unintended consequences that can do serious, and at times irreparable harm to people. Although we would like to think that we can always learn from our mistakes, it sometimes happens that our mistakes are so serious that they prevent all future learning from occurring. If a child decides to stop a bullet with his hand, and if he is so unfortunate that he is killed, then, of course, there is no more that can be said about learning, not learning, or anything else for him. Others may be able to learn something from an individual who mistakenly thought he could stop a bullet, but that is essentially beside the point.

If we realize that we may have to live with some of our mistakes, then we should carefully choose both the problem situations in which we are willing to test new ideas and the ideas to be tested. Although progress may be greatly aided by bold new solutions to problems, we should not deceive ourselves into thinking that all new solutions are necessarily better than the ones we already know; a new solution to a problem may well be more mistaken than the ones we presently know. And if we are dealing with problem situations which require that we act in the world, then we may make mistakes that do permanent harm. Thus, before testing new solutions to a problem, we should try to weigh the risks and potentially unintended consequences that might result from an innovative idea.

The evaluation of risks involved in different problem situations is extremely important for the classroom, because the range of problems that people may work on in school can vary greatly. Although we may not want to restrict children from merely thinking about such problems as stopping a bullet with their hand, we should set up rules for when and how to test new solutions to problems.[15] No school should allow or encourage its members to haphazardly test all suggested solutions to a problem, and it is only sane to apply sensible rules and regulations to the testing of innovative ideas.

BEING OPEN ABOUT DECISIONS AND MISTAKES

The third point to discuss in relationship to the problem of studying mistakes is that we should encourage people to expose their decisions to others, since we often need the help of others in order to uncover our mistakes. Individuals are often uncritical of the ideas they favor, and everyone can be greatly aided by the criticisms and suggestions of others.[16] Also, when we expose our decisions to others, learning from mistakes becomes efficient: if we can inform others of the mistakes we have made, it may not be necessary for them to make the same mistakes.

Discovering our mistakes is often a very difficult task, and individuals may not readily identify their mistakes. However, when groups of people attempt to discover mistakes, there is no reason always to identify certain mistakes with particular individuals. Specifically, if someone mistakenly suggests that the earth is shaped like a thin pancake, there is no need to ridicule him or view him and his mistakes as one. On the contrary, it is often both possible and desirable to totally disassociate people from the mistakes they make.

At times it is necessary and reasonable to find out who is responsible for a mistake. For example, if we assume that it is a mistake to shoot another person, and if a person is shot then it is reasonable to want to find out who is responsible for the shooting. Nevertheless, the problem of assigning responsibility for a mistake, and the problem of identifying a mistake, are two different problems.[17] We do not always have to identify a mistake with certain individuals, and sometimes it is unnecessary and irrelevant to do this.

VIEWING MISTAKES IMPERSONALLY AND OBJECTIVELY

People can view their own mistakes and those of others in an impersonal sense. We can talk about a mistake without any reference to personalities; in doing this we objectify the mistake.[18] This is important, since identifying individuals with particular mistakes is often not only an obstacle which prevents improvement but also is liable to cause people unnecessary pain.

Mistakes are often difficult to discuss. At times they cause individuals a great deal of embarrassment, discomfort, and the possibility of ridicule. It may be childish to be embarrassed by many of the mistakes we make. If we could take a truly positive view of our mistakes, we might find that there are such things as good mistakes; [19] the mistaken ideas suggested by such great scientists as Newton and Copernicus are not things that we should disdain these scientists for; these "mistakes" deserve our praise and admiration because they were imaginative ideas which helped us improve our understanding of the world, and without which Einstein's theories would most likely not have evolved.

Until people are willing to view mistakes in a quite positive light, it is probably better for us to disassociate mistakes from particular individuals. Even if we are able to view mistakes in a generally positive way, we should try to avoid confusing the source of a mistake with the mistake itself.

USING HUMAN ENERGY TO AVOID MISTAKES

The fifth point I would like to discuss is that we should concentrate our energies on avoiding future mistakes rather than on regretting past ones or fearing new ones. Some may think that I have been suggesting that individuals should dwell on old mistakes and fear making future ones. But I mean quite the opposite. Rather than dwell on old mistakes or fear making new ones, we should try to understand our mistakes in order to improve ourselves.

If we accept the notion that mistakes are an inevitable part of life, then some of our human energy should be used to reflect on past mistakes and possible future ones. Thus, it is desirable to ask the question, "How can human energies best be used in relationship to mistakes?" My answer to this question is that we should try to use human energy to understand our past and present mistakes so that we can offer better solutions to our problems.

It is important to realize that no one can change the situations or circumstances in which past mistakes have been made: we can

never change or manipulate the past into what we would like it to
have been. Nor can we totally control or manipulate the future
into what we would like it to be. Although people know intellectually that they cannot manipulate the past and the future, they
may still chose to regret the past and fear the future. But doing
this changes or improves nothing. And regretting our past mistakes
may well become an obstacle for improvement, since we then use
our energies in ways that prevent change; also, if we use our energies to fear future mistakes, we may become immobile and afraid
of all change and thus preclude any possibility of improvement.

I do not mean to suggest that people should spend all their
time thinking about past and future mistakes. Although I believe
it is desirable for people to spend some time making decisions
about which of their actions and ideas are mistaken, I also recommend that people think about ways to correct old mistakes. Since
I am for improvement, action, and decisiveness, I would not wish
to see people become stagnated or stifled by their mistakes. What
we need is a philosophy that can help us use mistakes to improve
human actions and get closer to the truth.

CURRICULUM AND THE STUDY OF MISTAKES

My sixth and final point is that the study of mistakes should be
allowed to become a respectable part of the school curriculum.[20]
This means that we should not expect or desire that children learn
only the latest and most fashionable ideas. On the contrary, we
should encourage and allow students to study problems or issues
from a historical perspective.

A major obstacle to making the study of mistakes an intricate
part of the school curriculum is the often asserted claim that there
is not enough time for children to learn the most useful and
worthwhile ideas available. Hence, many curriculum developers
seek to limit the number of ideas that children are exposed to in
the classroom. It is very common for curriculum developers to
suggest that children should be taught only "worthy" ideas;[21]
since mistaken ideas are usually viewed as unworthy, they are
often eliminated from the curriculum.

The notion of limiting the school curriculum to include only worthy ideas is academically and intellectually inadequate—it gives children the erroneous impression that problems have only one solution. But the history of most academic fields suggests that there is much conflict and disagreement over how to solve problems. It is interesting to note that consensus does not always exist among all the experts in a field of study.[22]

Problems are open-ended situations which can be studied historically; when children study the mistaken solutions to a problem, they have the opportunity to understand that problems are dynamic, rather than static, situations. It is desirable for children to be aware that problem situations are dynamic, since human knowledge can grow and improve only through change.

CONCLUDING REMARKS

In this paper I have made concrete suggestions about how to incorporate the study of mistakes into an educational program. These suggestions can be summarized as follows: (1) we should encourage people to be clear about what problem a decision or action is related to; (2) we should try, whenever possible, to control and choose the kind of mistakes we are willing to make in varying problem situations; (3) we should be willing to expose our decisions, actions, and possible mistakes to others; (4) we should try to objectify our mistakes and view them in an impersonal sense; (5) we should concentrate our energies on avoiding future mistakes rather than on regretting past ones or fearing new ones; and (6) we should allow problems to be studied historically so that mistakes can become a respectable part of the school curriculum.

These suggestions represent a beginning solution to the problem of studying mistakes. However, I do not think that this solution could or should be incorporated into all ongoing educational programs. Unfortunately, our present prejudicial attitudes toward mistakes are too strong to be readily changed. Too, educational and social change are very complex phenomena, and it is probably wise to test new ideas and policies by means of pilot programs. What kinds of changes will we have to make in order to develop experimental educational programs where people can be open and honest about mistakes? Can groups of people learn how to deal with their own mistakes and those of others without feeling guilty or fearful? Can we control the area and the likely kinds of mistakes in those areas so that students and teachers can freely make mistakes? Hopefully, questions such as these will seem reasonable and worthy of serious consideration in light of the ideas presented in this chapter.

NOTES

1. For an introduction to many of the ideas associated with viewing knowledge as falliable see the following: John Stuart Mill, *On Liberty* (New York: Appleton-Century-Crofts, 1947), pp. 15-54; Bertrand Russell, *Philosophical Essays* (New York: Simon and Schuster, 1968), pp. 79-111; Karl R. Popper, *Conjectures and Refutations: The Growth of Scientific Knowledge* (New York: Basic Books, 1962), pp. 3-30.

2. The notion that people should discuss the questions used to formulate a problem is discussed throughout the works of Karl R. Popper and his school. Popperians often endorse the notion that a question well put and explained is half answered. For examples and statements about the importance of discussing questions and formulations of problems see the following: Karl R. Popper, *Objective Knowledge* (London: Oxford University Press, 1974), pp. 1-31; Joseph Agassi, "The Logic of Scientific Inquiry," *Synthese* 26 (1974): 498-514; Ronald Swartz, "Problems and Their Possible Uses in Educational Programs," *Philosophy of Education 1973: Proceedings of the Twenty-ninth Annual Meeting of the Philosophy of Education Society*, ed. Brian Crittenden (Edwardsville, Ill.: Philosophy of Education Society, 1973), pp. 135-45. At this time I would like to thank Jerome Schenwar and Jerry Taft for their helpful comments on my early formulations of the ideas discussed in this paper.

3. For some of my early ideas about the importance of studying mistakes see Swartz, "Problems and Their Possible Uses," pp. 138-41. Also refer to Popper, *Conjectures and Refutations*, pp. 238-40.

4. A good example of how contemporary educators recognize the importance of mistakes for learning can be found in Jerome Bruner, *The Process of Education* (New York: Vintage Books, 1960), p. 65. As Bruner states, "effective intuitive thinking . . . requires a willingness to make honest mistakes in the effort to solve problems." It is important to note that Bruner, and others who have talked about the role of mistakes in the learning process, have not really developed systematic ideas about mistakes, but have instead merely tacitly dealt with the problem of studying mistakes.

5. See the following: Ronald Swartz, "Education as Entertainment and Irresponsibility in the Classroom," *Science Education* 58 no. 1 (January–March 1974): 119-26; "Some Criticisms of the Distribution of Authority in the Classroom," *Focus on Learning* 4, no. 1 (Spring–Summer 1974): 33-40; "Schooling

and Responsibility," *Science Education* 59, no. 3 (July–September 1975): 409–12.

6. Refer to the references in note 2.

7. Refer to the references in note 1.

8. For a detailed summary of arguments which explain why a fallibilist thinks it is wrong to rely on authorities see Charles Sanders Peirce, "The Scientific Attitude and Fallibilism," *Philosophical Writings of Peirce*, ed. Justus Buchler (New York: Dover Publications, 1955), pp. 54–59.

9. A good summary statement about how fallibilism is associated with optimistic notions such as the advancement of knowledge can be found in Karl R. Popper, *The Open Society and Its Enemies*, vol. 2 (New York: Harper and Row, 1962), pp. 374–76.

10. See Popper, *Conjuctures and Refutations*, p. vii.

11. The notion of viewing truth as an unattainable goal which is beyond human grasp is discussed in the following: Popper, *Objective Knowledge*, pp. 191–205, and Russell, *Philosophical Essays*, p. 109. In viewing truth as an unattainable goal, Popper and Russell have tried to disassociate their view of fallibilism from pragmatists such as Peirce, James, and Dewey. For an interesting discussion on why the pragmatic notion of "truth" is unsatisfactory for some fallibilists see Bertrand Russell, *A History of Western Philosophy* (New York: Simon and Schuster, 1945), pp. 819–28. It is important to note that both Popper and Russell view truth in an absolute and unchangeable sense and that they reject the notion of a relative truth or a truth that changes over time.

12. A discussion on the need to make decisions in spite of the fact that we can never be certain about our ideas can be found in Michael Polanyi, *Personal Knowledge* (New York: Harper and Row, 1962), pp. 269–98. Polanyi is not usually viewed as a fallibilist, and his ideas are often seen as a criticism of contemporary fallibilism. One of the major problems with Polanyi's criticism of fallibilism is that he does not separate the notion of making a decision from the notion of being certain about the decisions that one makes. If these two notions can be separated, then fallibilists can make decisions which they are uncertain about. For a discussion on how a fallibilist views the decision-making process see Mill, *On Liberty*, p. 21.

13. For a discussion about the importance of being clear about our problem situations see Karl R. Popper, *The Logic of Scientific Discovery* (New York: Harper and Row, 1962), p. 16. Also, refer to note 2.

14. The notion of being careful about choosing one's problem situation is most important for areas in which people plan actions. That is, we can make mistakes in our theoretical understanding of the world, and these mistakes may not bring about irreparable harm. However, if we decide to act on our ideas, then we have to deal with the consequences of our actions, and these consequences may cause us harm. For a discussion about the distinction between theoretical and practical problems see Bertrand Russell, *Sceptical Essays* (New York: Barnes and Noble, 1963), pp. 32–37.

15. See Swartz, "Education as Entertainment and Irresponsibility in the Classroom," pp. 123-24.

16. Refer to notes 2 and 13.

17. See Popper, *Conjectures and Refutations*, p. 24. Also see Stephenie G. Edgerton, "The Sociology of Knowledge Revisited," *Studies in Philosophy and Education* 4, no. 3 (Spring 1966): 338.

18. When mistakes are objectified they are viewed in a public and social context rather than in a private and individual sense. The idea of making our mistakes public and social is similar to the notion of objectifying the experiences that scientists use to test their theories. That is, some philosophers of science have suggested that experiences can be objectified if they are written as statements describing an observable phenomenon. For an introductory discussion about objectifying scientific observations see Carl G. Hempel, *Philosophy of Natural Science* (Englewood Cliffs, N.J.: Prentice-Hall, 1966), pp. 30-32. A more technical discussion of these ideas can be found in Popper, *The Logic of Scientific Discovery*, pp. 100-105.

19. For an interesting discussion on how modern European languages associate mistakes with negative ideas see Joseph Agassi, "Towards an Historiography of Science," *History and Theory* 2 (1963), p. 54.

20. Refer to note 3.

21. For a discussion on the need to select worthy ideas for the curriculum see Arno A. Bellack, "What Knowledge Is of Most Worth?" *The Changing Secondary School Curriculum Readings,* ed. William M. Alexander (New York: Holt, Rinehart and Winston, 1967), pp. 221-34.

22. See Karl R. Popper, "Normal Science and Its Dangers," *Criticism and the Growth of Knowledge,* ed. Imre Lakatos and Alan Musgrave (Cambridge: Cambridge University Press, 1970), pp. 51-58. Also see James Hullett, "Which Structure?" *Educational Theory* 24, no. 1 (Winter 1974): 68-72. Finally, refer to the references in notes 3 and 12.

CHAPTER 3

Against Learning*

HENRY J. PERKINSON

EDUCATIONAL AUTHORITARIANISM

The title is catchy but somewhat inaccurate. I am not really against learning. I am against construing the educational process as learning. And I'm against the notion of the school as a learning center. But most of all, I'm against casting the teacher as a promoter of learning.

By "learning" I mean the acquisition of skills, ideas, and dispositions. Now, why am I against teachers promoting the acquisition of skills, ideas, and dispositions?

Because casting the teacher into this role focuses attention on the techniques of promoting learning and thus converts education into a technocratic enterprise. "How can I get students to learn?" is a technocratic question. It directs the teacher to search out the appropriate means for producing some predetermined end: a human being who has learned something. As technocrats, teachers assume that what students learn (or are supposed to learn) under

---

* This paper previously appeared in *Focus on Learning* (Fall–Winter 1975), pp. 5–19. The paper presented here contains a few minor changes from the original version.

their promotion is true, good, and desirable; indeed, they have to become dogmatic about such things—a "good" teacher is always able and ready to defend and justify the learning he or she promotes. What is even more distressing is that "good" teachers pass this dogmatism on to their students by insisting that they, too, defend what they have learned: "Always be able to explain why what you have learned is true, or good, or desirable."

So, casting the teacher into the role of promoter of learning converts education into a technocratic enterprise, and this fosters authoritarian teachers. As I understand it, authoritarianism prevents the growth or advancement of knowledge; hence, I'm against it. This authoritarianism manifests itself in the ways educators have responded to the query: "How can I get students to learn?"

One of these responses, recently labeled "the problem of the match," [1] consists of "matching" or "fitting" what is to be learned to the learner himself. For centuries educators have tried to work out the principles for matching. Comenius wrestled with it,[2] John Dewey saw it as the central problem of progressive education; [3] and most present-day teachers see it as their main task.

This notion of matching is best described through the "building-block" metaphor of education. According to this metaphor, the teacher who seeks to promote learning must "build" upon what the student already knows, after first assuring that the student does have a "firm foundation" of learning. At this point, the teacher confronts the problem of the match, or fit: the teacher must discover, manufacture, or create "blocks" of learning—of correct size, density, and weight—to "fit" into the edifice of learning the child already has. These "blocks of learning" are the bits and pieces of the various matters the teacher is supposed to get across to, or into, the student.

The attempt to find the fit is only one of the proposed authoritarian "solutions" to the question of how to promote learning. A second, and related, authoritarian solution is the attempt to "motivate" the student. Motivation is related, for, even if the block of learning is the correct fit for the student's edifice of learning, he must see that it fits, he must accept it, get it; he must want it: therefore, the teacher must motivate him to learn. We can classify most theories of motivation as either "push" or "pull" theories. The pull theories use some kind of carrot (purpose, value, or need), and the push theories some kind of pitchfork (drive, motive, or stimulus) to get the student, one way or the other, to learn what he is supposed to learn.[4]

Many modern educational theorists from Rousseau through Dewey to A. S. Neill and the so-called romantic critics have turned against the traditional ways of matching and motivating. The traditional ways, they have insisted, are authoritarian because teachers predetermine what is to be taught and force students to learn it. In so predetermining what the students are supposed to learn, these critics continue, the teachers rarely find the fit; and since what they predetermine is usually dull, dreary, irrelevant, and useless, they often fail to motivate the students to learn. The result, these critics observe, is readily apparent: frustrated teachers become more authoritarian; students, more restive, apathetic, and resistant. And when, as has occurred since midcentury, more and more children come to the schools and stay there longer and longer, this authoritarianism becomes more pronounced, and the response from the students becomes more poignant and dramatic.

The solution to the question of how to promote learning put forth by many of these modern critics consists of having students learn only those things they are interested in. They urge teachers and schools to become child centered. They talk about teachers serving as "facilitators" of learning.[5] In keeping with this prescription, we today witness teachers using the inquiry or discovery approach and schools providing open classrooms, or even open and free schools, methods, and arrangements that allow students to learn what is of interest to them.

Yet, even if the modern critics have their dreams fulfilled, even if they lick the problem of the fit and the problem of motivation by having the students learn what they find exciting, interesting, and useful, there is still a problem: a problem with what is learned. For much of what is learned is false, mistaken, inadequate, even harmful. This is so of our students and of us, too. Whether we learn in a teacher-centered curriculum or a child-centered one, whether we learn in school or out, under the guidance of a teacher or on our own, we cannot insure that what we learn is true, or even correct, right, good, appropriate, or satisfactory. Human beings are not infallible, so what they learn cannot be perfect. We cannot devise ways of learning for ourselves or for our students that will guarantee the truth of our ideas, the adequacy of our skills, or the goodness of our dispositions. This fact suggests that the modern critics have not fully unveiled the authoritarianism inherent in the educational process today. So long as we construe education as learning, the school as a learning center, and teachers as promoters of learning, we are constructing an authoritarian enterprise. Child-centered education merely shifts the locus of final authority from the teacher to the student. What the student learns here is supposedly true, right, good, or appropriate because it comes out of his own experience. But this obviously won't do; it is just as authoritarian as saying that what the student learns is true because the teacher (or the textbook or the expert) says it is true.

The modern advocates of student-centered education claim that students learn more readily and effectively those things in which they are interested.[6] But it is precisely for this reason that student-centered education is bad education. This kind of education develops a strong, often unrefutable, faith in what has been learned. "I know it's true; I experienced it!" What is learned becomes permanently a part of the learner, which is another way of saying that a person cannot improve his learning. He is committed to what he has learned; indeed, we can say he identifies himself with it. He is what he has learned. To criticize his ideas, the skills, the dispositions he has is to attack him. Thus, the learner will resist criticism, guard what he "knows" against attack, hold on to his learning at all costs. In short, his learning will not advance; it will stagnate.

Teachers who seek to promote or facilitate learning, whether they employ the traditional teacher-centered approach or the modern child-centered approach, convert education into an authoritarian enterprise. The more successful they are at promoting learning, the more they insure that what is learned will not advance or improve.

EDUCATION WITHOUT FINAL AUTHORITIES

If we are ever to eliminate authoritarianism from education, we cannot merely shift the locus of final authority from the teacher to the student; we must completely get rid of the notion of final authorities. And this suggests that we must construe education differently.

What would an education without final authorities be like? This construction of education would direct us away from technocratic questions about how to promote learning to focus on questions about the worth of what is learned. Once we try to ascertain the worth of what is learned without appeal to any final authority, we discover that we must abandon the notion of justification, facing up to the fact that without final authorities we cannot ever demonstrate that what we learn or what our students learn is true, good, or appropriate. How, then, can we ascertain the worth of our learning? We can do this by approaching it critically, trying to find out what is wrong with it. Thus, we can compare our ideas, skills, and dispositions—or those of our students—with other ideas, skills and dispositions, thereby revealing ways in which one, or the other, is inadequate or wrong. This critical, or ecological, approach leads to the refinement or modification of learning.

To construe education in this way is to construe the enterprise as human, not technical—an enterprise rooted in our human condition of fallibility. Education becomes a modest endeavor, an endeavor to create better ideas, skills, and dispositions—not an attempt to impose justified ones.

This conception of education as improvement construes the process itself as one of evolution or growth. Now, of course, many educators have construed education this way; but all such constructions have been Lamarckian rather than Darwinian. According to Lamark's (discredited) theory, evolution takes place through the transmission of acquired characteristics to offspring. Because educators persisted in equating education with learning, they inevitably adopted a Lamarckian theory of human growth. Thus, most educators have construed the student, or his mind, as a tabula rasa—a blank slate, or an empty vessel, bereft of knowledge. The student (or his mind or his knowledge) grows through the acquisition of knowledge that the teacher transmits directly, via instruction, or indirectly, via providing appropriate experiences.

Darwin's theory of evolution is quite different. According to him, evolution took place through natural selection: organisms produce offspring that in some small ways differ from themselves; the environment (nature) selects and rejects as unfit those that develop in inadequate ways. Thus, the unfit do not survive: they have no offspring.

Some philosophers of science, notably Sir Karl Popper, have adopted the Darwinian theory of evolution in explaining how science advances and grows.[7] Science, they say, grows through the continual criticism of existing and proposed scientific theories. Criticism identifies errors and inadequacies, leading to the refinement of the theories in light of the unrefuted criticism. To paraphrase the theory of natural selection, we can say that science grows through the process of submitting its theories to an environment of criticism which selects and rejects as unfit those that are falsified. I am suggesting that we apply this Darwinian construction of the growth of science to the educational process itself and get rid of the Lamarckian theory of growth that dominates contemporary educational thought.

The Darwinian conception of education rejects the notion of the student as a tabula rasa. That is, just as biological evolution presupposes that each newborn generation contains mutations that will be selected and rejected, so evolutionary education presupposes that students possess learning. According to this conception, learning is not synonymous with education; it is the starting point. The process of education is the refinement, the improvement of what one has already learned. Education presupposes learning.[8]

I think it is important to note that the Lamarckian theory of growth does simulate what really happens according to the Darwinian theory. That is, as all teachers know, students do come to school possessed of learning, most of which is wrong, inadequate, inchoate, and fallacious. Teachers then traditionally proceed to present ideas, demonstrate skills, and praise dispositions different from, and purportedly superior to, those that the students already have. As a result, the students, with varying degrees of success, attempt to refine their own ideas, skills, and dispositions because the models and exemplars presented by the teacher have revealed the inadequacy of their own ideas, skills, or dispositions. So it looks as if the student is acquiring knowledge transmitted by the teacher—in accordance with the Lamarckian theory of growth— while in point of fact the student is refining or modifying his knowledge in light of the criticism tacitly professed.

Thus, the Lamarckian theory of growth approximates the Darwinian one. But what is wrong with this Lamarckian construction of education is that it stymies further growth. According to it, successful education consists of the acquisition of the approved, true, correct knowledge: knowledge justified by some final authority. This fosters a dogmatic or authoritarian attitude toward the knowledge acquired. For if the learner believes that the knowledge he possesses is "true" (i.e., justified), then he will be inclined to secure it against change, against modification, against refinement. The knowledge will not grow.

The Darwinian construction of evolutionary education makes explicit the spring of growth: knowledge advances through selection and rejection of errors and inadequacies in the knowledge we already possess. Through discovering how and in what ways our ideas, skills, and dispositions are false, inadequate and bad, we can set about refining, changing, or replacing them. The new ones we create are better than the old insofar as they lack the recognized defects of the old. And since we can never make them perfect, we can continually improve them, so long as we approach them critically. This means that education need never end. Thus, instead of authoritarianism and dogmatism, the Darwinian construction of evolutionary education fosters an awareness of human fallibility. If successful, rather than protecting knowledge and defending it against change, a Darwinian approach to education leads students to the conscious effort to improve knowledge.

THE NEW ROLE OF THE TEACHER AND THE
SCHOOL

If we adopt the Darwinian construction of evolutionary education, then what about the function of the school? What about the
role of the teacher? The school will no longer be construed as a
center of learning. It is, after all, somewhat presumptuous to cast
the school as a center for learning, since learning occurs in many
places, not just in school; it occurs in many ways, not just under
the guidance of a teacher. Learning is ubiquitous and endless; it
never ceases. Learning happens; it happens all the time. But we do
need a place where we can test the worth of what we have learned,
a place where we can criticize so that we can improve. So, if we
adopt the Darwinian conception of evolutionary education, we
can construct the school as a center for criticism—a critical agency.

And the teacher? No longer the promoter of learning, the
teacher will now simply try to help students improve knowledge
by helping them to probe, to test, to experiment with—to criticize—the knowledge they already have. Perhaps the best way to
convey this construction of the role of the teacher and the function of the school is to cast it in a new metaphor.

I suggest we adopt the closet-cleaning metaphor. Every student
has a closet full of ideas, skills, and dispositions that he has accumulated in the course of his life. But much of what he has accumulated is false, mistaken, erroneous, mythical, inadequate, and
may even be harmful. The educational process is one of closet
cleaning. The teacher helps the student clean his own closet by
helping him to criticize and test the worth of the ideas, skills, and
dispositions he has accumulated. But it is not the teacher's job to
replenish the closet. The teacher does not have a pile of official
wisdom, or guaranteed skills, or approved dispositions to give, sell,
install, or foist off on the student. The teacher is not a closet
stuffer, not a promoter of learning. The teacher's task is the liqui-
dation of ignorance, the elimination of false, mistaken, and inadequate ideas, skills, and dispositions.[9]

The closet-cleaner teacher, unlike the building-block teacher,
has no concern with the matter of the "fit," nor with motivation.

These problems emerged from the theory that the teacher's role was the promotion of knowledge; once we abandon it, they disappear. The closet-cleaner teacher is not trying to impose anything on the student. She is trying to help him to improve what he has already learned.

So far, I have argued that to construe education as learning, schools as places where learning takes place, and teachers as promoters of learning is to construct education as an authoritarian enterprise, with schools and teachers becoming manipulators of the young. Even the modern child-centered educational theorists, insofar as they equate education with learning, are constructing an authoritarian enterprise. I have suggested that we can avoid authoritarianism by construing education as evolution or improvement, schools as critical agencies, and teachers as critics.

I will now sketch how a teacher could function as a critic. What follows is not a scheme for a total, nor even a radical transformation of our existing educational systems. The changes I propose in the role of the teacher can occur within the present arrangements in most schools. I see no necessity to start altering the structure, the organization, or the curriculum, although introducing this change in the role of the teacher will result in changes in all of them. My intention here is to initiate educational reform by urging educators to begin with what can be changed immediately: the way the teacher construes his or her role in the educative process.

IMPROVING SKILLS

Much of what we now teach in schools consists of skills: reading, writing, arithmetic, as well as typing, spelling, swimming, dancing, and music. Furthermore, some teach the social sciences, like history, or the physical sciences, like physics, as skills: in these classrooms, students learn to do history or physics.

The basic assumption of the closet-cleaner teacher is that the student already possesses skills. He possesses them in a rudimentary, primitive, or gross way that he must now begin to refine. Thus, the young child in the first grade has mathematical skills: he can count, or separate one entity or unit from another; he can draw lines, curved ones and ones less curved. He has reading skills: he can decode or read signals or signs or symbols; he can decode or "read" another's face to tell the other's mood; he can decode or read traffic signals, he can read picture books. He has writing skills: he can make marks and zigs and zags with a pencil or crayon. He has musical skills: he can sing, hum; he can bang a drum, make sounds on a piano. In short, all children, even the youngest, possess skills—motor skills, manual skills, and cognitive skills—in some gross form.

In order to improve, the student must refine his own skills; he must alter, change, or modify what he can already do. To help him do this, the closet-cleaner teacher first elicits, or educes, the skills he now has. The next step is to help him recognize the inadequacy of that skill. Finally, the teacher encourages him to modify the skill and try again.

There are at least two ways of eliciting a skill from a student. One is by confronting him with a problem—a math problem, say, or a problem in physics, or even a passage to read, or a paragraph to type. A second way to do it is to ask the student to imitate a model—a drawing or a painting, for example, or the movements of a swimmer, or some arithmetical calculation, or the spelling of a word.

Once the student has exhibited his skill, the teacher's task is to criticize it, to help him discover the inadequacies of the errors. This sounds harsh and debilitating—even fearsome. Yet it need not be any of these things at all. Everything depends upon the mood and atmosphere established by the teacher and the mode of interacting with the student. The teacher must demonstrate that he or she is there to help him, not to grade him; there to help him improve his skills, not to embarrass him. The teacher's credentials or warrant for helping the student improve a skill is not the ability to perform that skill. No, it is the ability to uncover and demonstrate the inadequacies in student's performances. The mathematics teacher need not be a master mathematician, nor the swimming teacher a champion swimmer, nor the drawing teacher a professional artist. For each, the warrant to teach is that the teacher is able to discover and point out inadequacies in the skills of those being taught. (When a teacher is no longer able to do this, then the student is ready for a new teacher.)

The closet-cleaner teacher does not approach the student as an authority but as a helpful critic. One modern educational theorist who partly shared this conception of the role of the teacher was Maria Montessori. With her so-called didactic materials, she provided a means both for eliciting the skills the child already possesses and for simultaneously criticizing them—helping him to discover the inadequacies of a specific skill.[10] The Montessori didactic materials are so constructed that they reveal to the child his mistakes. Thus, for example, if he places one or more dowels in the wrong holes, the remaining dowels will not fit in the remaining holes; the materials themselves make manifest his errors. This control of error built into the materials spares the child the possible embarrassment and fear of being told by the teacher that he has made a mistake. Moreover, these didactic materials are graduated in difficulty so that the kinds of discrimination called for are ever more precise. By providing a wide variety of these didactic materials for the children to choose from, the Montessori classroom permits them to improve the skills they already possess. All of Montessori's work was with young children. But it is obvious that schools could develop arrangements for teaching many different kinds of skills—typing, swimming, painting—that would incorporate the principles inherent in her didactic materials.

Maria Montessori presented her didactic materials as means to promote the learning skills—learning how to read, calculate, write, and so on. She was not concerned, as is the closet-cleaner teacher, with the continual improvement of all skills. She appeared never to ask how we can continually improve, although obviously we can all continue to improve our linguistic, mathematic, and writing skills—improving them indefinitely. Although she herself paid no heed to this question, Montessori actually incorporated the means for continual improvement in her so-called didactic materials: the discovery of error and inadequacy. Now, the teacher who takes on the function of continually improving skills must move beyond Maria Montessori's concern—a concern shared by most teachers—merely to promote the learning of skills. To do this, the teacher must help the student realize right from the beginning that all skills can be continually improved.

One way to do this is through the study of the historical improvement or evolution of the various skills human beings have acquired—a development that came about as human beings continually discovered the inadequacies of their existing skills and continually refined them in light of these discoveries. Since the stress in this historical study will be on man's fallibility—his inability to develop perfect skills—the focus will be on problem raising, not problem solving. That is, the teacher will direct students to the ways and conditions under which earlier skills broke down. Thus, students will see that throughout history people have continually developed skills that have in one way or another proved to be inadequate. But they will also see that once he discovered an inadequacy, man has refined his skills, thus improving them.

The history of the skill in question helps the student to see that there is no final proper way to perform the skill. Such history helps him to see that men have tried a lot of inadequate ways. This historical survey need not take up too much time; only enough so that students recognize that man can continually improve his skills—linguistic, literary, mathematical, or whatever; second, the student will also come to recognize that the way to improvement is through the continual search for inadequacies and the continual testing of those skills. This recognition of the possibility of continual improvement is merely propaedeutic to the central task of the teacher of skills: the continual improvement of the skills each student already possesses.

In summary, the closet-cleaner teacher who wants to improve skills goes through three phases. First, the teacher elicits the skills the student already possesses. One can do this in at least two ways: by asking the student to imitate a specific model, or by presenting him with a problem to solve which will call upon the skill in question. The second task is to criticize the skill, helping the student to recognize the inadequacies of it. (Sometimes, as with Montessori's didactic materials, the teacher can combine the first, or eliciting phase, with the second, or critical phase.) In the third phase, the teacher persuades the student to try again. Here the mode or manner of the teacher is all-important. One must not make the student fearful. The approach to him should not be that of a judge nor of a grader, but rather that of a helper.

The upshot of this kind of education will be that the student becomes expert in the various skills, but more important, he becomes a student of those skills, concerned with their continual improvement, and possessed of the way to that improvement: continual criticism.

THE IMPROVEMENT OF IDEAS

Many teachers, especially those in secondary schools, have the task of teaching the young about man and his physical and social environment—its past and present. They do this through a variety of subjects: history, the social and behavioral sciences, and the physical sciences. The closet-cleaner teacher who takes the educational task to be the improvement of ideas assumes that students already do have ideas about man and the physical and social world he inhabits. Students in the secondary schools have closets full of ideas, theories, and notions; perhaps they are fuzzy ideas, undeveloped theories, and vague notions—but they have them nonetheless. The closet-cleaner teacher also makes a second assumption about students: that they are able to argue and able to understand arguments. As Piaget has demonstrated, this inferential thinking does not develop until adolescence.[11] Therefore, although elementary school teachers may want to teach the social and physical sciences, they will not be able to function as closet cleaners. Insofar as students are incapable of inferential thinking, instruction in these subjects in the elementary grades does not improve the students' ideas; it merely imposes ideas on them. (This I take to be a good argument for not teaching the physical and social sciences in the elementary school.)

After making the assumptions that the student does have ideas, what does the closet-cleaner teacher do? Maybe it is best first to note what the closet-cleaner teacher does not do: the closet-cleaner teacher doesn't impose the subject matter on the student. Rather, the teacher presents the subject matter for the student's criticism, never asking him to accept the ideas presented, but to criticize them. The closet-cleaner teacher invites the student to engage in a critical dialogue.

Imagine the school as a large department store—a free store, if you will—each department stocked with the traditional wisdom of each discipline or subject matter. To it comes the student, bringing with him (he cannot do otherwise) his own closet full of his accumulated learnings. There the teacher confronts him with the ideas, notions, theories contained in the traditional wisdom of the subject matters. This encounter permits the student to do three things: (1) to compare his own ideas, theories, and notions with those presented; (2) to assess the worth of his ideas, and (3) to refine them in light of the assessment.

Here the teacher's initial task is to see to it that a critical encounter takes place. One of the most common obstacles to a critical encounter crops up when the teacher presents the traditional wisdom of the subject matter as a finished product—as final knowledge. When a teacher presents history or physics or biology as a logically ordered system, he or she conveys to the student that there is a body of true knowledge called history, another called physics, another called biology. Confronted with this "true knowledge," the students can do naught but accept it (or ignore it): they will not encounter it critically.

Instead of presenting fully worked out logical systems, the closet-cleaner teachers will present their various subject matters as conjectures—conjectures made by fallible men in answer to specific problems. Students, right from the start, must recognize that scientists create science, that psychologists create psychology, physicists create physics, and historians create history. Moreover, right from the start, students recognize that they are students of problems, not of answers. And, probably most important, right from the start students recognize that the problems they are studying are problems about knowledge; that is, problems about the previous conjectures men have made.[12]

All this might be made clearer by noting the assumptions that the closet-cleaner teacher makes about the various subject matters. The teacher assumes that man creates his knowledge. But each man does not start off anew. He inherits the knowledge men have created in the past. This knowledge, all of which is conjectural, cannot be perfect—it was created by fallible men. But it can be improved by discovering its inadequacies and eliminating the errors it contains. However, this improved knowledge cannot be perfect either; it will contain new problems or modified versions of the old problems. These new problems can be revealed through the critical scrutiny of the "improved knowledge." In brief, then, students of the closet-cleaner teacher recognize that all the various subject matters have histories, and each history is the story of the continual discovery of the various inadequacies contained in man's successive conjectures about himself and the universe in which he lives. In order to help students recognize this construction of the subject matters, the closet-cleaner teacher will begin with a historical approach. Let me sketch how the science teacher might use this approach.

Taking a specific conjecture (C_1) made in the past by some scientist about some phenomenon in the universe, the teacher shows how it was an attempt to solve a problem contained in a previous "scientific" conjecture (C). The previous conjecture (C) had proved to be inadequate; it led to disappointed expectations. The new conjecture (C_1) represents an improvement insofar as it eliminates those disappointed expectations; or, we might say it is a better theory because it does not contain the errors revealed in the previous conjecture (C).

By approaching the work of scientists historically, the teacher shows how science advances: through scientists making conjectures and then discovering the errors in those conjectures. Thus, the teacher will show how, in time, the new conjecture (C_1) also proved to be inadequate. It, too, led to (other) disappointed expectations, resulting in a revised, or new, conjecture (C_2) to overcome the problems contained in, or caused by, the previous conjecture (C_1). The teacher continues this historical pattern up to the present:

Problem emerging from inadequate conjectured theory (C)
↓
New conjectured theory (C_1)
↓
Problem emerging from inadequate conjectured theory (C_1)
↓
New conjectured theory (C_2)

In tracing the history of scientific theories about a specific phenomenon, the teacher ultimately confronts the students with the present-day conjectured theory or theories that have emerged as attempts to solve or overcome the problems uncovered in previous conjectures. At this point, the teacher invites the students to engage these latest conjectures critically. To facilitate a critical encounter, the teacher can present these present-day theories in an invitational mode: "These latest theories cannot be perfect; they, too, were created by fallible men. Let's see what's wrong with them."

This invitation to a critical engagement constitutes an attempt to initiate the students into the work of scientists; specifically, it is an invitation to participate in the critical tradition of a particular research program or field of inquiry. The student now becomes a participant in the advancement of knowledge.

At this juncture, the student begins to "act like a scientist." For the closet-cleaner teacher, this means that the student will attempt to criticize the present-day theories or ideas, to find out what is wrong with them, or to ascertain their limitations. The teacher will invite the students to present their own arguments against the conjectures of the scientists; will ask them to devise and carry out experiments to test the conjectures; and will suggest they do laboratory, library, or field research to probe them.

After the student presents his criticisms of the latest conjectures of the scientists, the teacher develops the critical encounter by engaging in critical dialogue with the student—criticizing his criticisms—not in order to grade or evaluate him but in order to help him recognize the inadequacies of his criticisms, to help him become a better critic. When criticising the student's criticisms, the teacher zeroes in on the educator's target: the closet full of ideas the student has about the world. The student's criticisms will emanate from his own ideas. So, by criticizing the student's criticisms, the teacher is actually trying to help him discover some of the inadequacies of his own ideas. The student, of course, must respond to these criticisms, criticizing them. This creates a critical dialogue.

The dialogue will uncover some of the limitations and weaknesses of some of the ideas in the student's closet. And the dialogue may also uncover some of the weaknesses and limitations in the conjectures of the scientists. The discovery of inadequacy leads to the reconstruction or refining of ideas: the advancement or improvement of knowledge. The critical dialogue initiates students as participants in the activity of advancing knowledge via criticism.

Here we must repeat that the concern of the teacher is with the improvement of the student's ideas, with finding out and helping the student to discover ways in which his ideas are inadequate. The student, on the other hand, is concerned with the improvement of the conjectures of the scientists, discovering ways in which the scientists' conjectures are inadequate. He is a postulant in the advancement of scientific knowledge. The teacher can help the student improve his own ideas only insofar as the student seriously and critically engages the conjectures of the scientists, for only in this way does he reveal and make public his own closet full of ideas—ideas then subject to criticisms by the teacher. This is not to say that the student will be unconcerned with the improvement of his own ideas, but as John Stuart Mill said of the pursuit of happiness, this is "only to be attained by not making it the direct end." Even though the student does want to improve his ideas, he cannot be sure which ones are inadequate, the ones on which he should focus. By focusing on the conjectures of the scientists, he directs himself to a historically significant area of inquiry, makes public his own ideas, and tests their adequacy.

The teacher and student can pursue the critical dialogue through continuing discussion and experiments or research projects, field trips, or whatever ways the participants decide. The refinement and improvement of the student's ideas in light of the inadequacies discovered through the critical dialogue is a task the student must perform himself. The improved ideas, too, will be open to criticism when, in a later critical dialogue, the student makes them public.

The closet-cleaner teacher of history and the social sciences will follow the same pattern as the teacher of science. But there are differences. History and the social sciences are not linear like the natural sciences. Modern historians and modern social and political theorists have not superseded the works of the ancients, as has occurred in the natural sciences. Therefore, the closet-cleaner teacher of history and the social sciences in the secondary school can plunder the past rather than present a linear progression of conjectures about man and society from the past to the present.

That is, in teaching these subjects, the teacher will confront the students with different interpretations of the past made by different historians, or different theories conjectured by different social theorists about a specific phenomenon. Then the teacher will invite the students to engage these conflicting interpretations and theories critically: "These two scholars say conflicting things about man, or society. They cannot both be correct. What criticisms can you make of their conjectures?"

Once again the teacher's concern is with the student's closet full of ideas—elicited by the criticisms he makes of the theories presented to him. By engaging his criticisms with criticisms, the teacher develops a critical dialogue that helps the student to discover the weaknesses, inadequacies, or limitations in his own ideas. Once again, the student is initiated into a research program or a field of inquiry where he becomes a postulant participant in the advancement of knowledge in that field. And in the very process of such initiation, the teacher helps him advance or improve his own closet full of ideas.

At this point, it may be well to confront a practical question: Can all students engage in critical dialogue? Isn't this method suitable for bright students only? Moreover, can a class of twenty (or thirty or forty!) students engage in critical dialogue?

These questions emerge from the very construction of education that I am arguing against in this paper. That is, to construe education as learning and the student's mind as a tabula rasa is to construct an approach to education that favors those who most readily learn, and those who have a large fund of information: so-called bright students. Bright students are easier to teach, easier to educate, and any teaching method or scheme to increase the speed of learning or the amount of learning that takes place always works best with the bright students.

But I have argued that we need not construe education as learning, as acquisition, nor students' minds as buckets to be filled. Nor need the teacher construe the task of education teleologically: getting some predetermined learning across to or into the student. We can construe education as the evolution or growth of knowledge or learning that the student already possesses. This construes the teacher's task historically: the refinement of the student's inadequate knowledge. To construe education this way is to overcome the prejudice in favor of the bright student, for *all* students—bright ones and ones not so bright—do possess knowledge. All can refine their present knowledge. The teacher must take all students' ideas, skills, and dispositions seriously, helping them to make them public without fear or anxiety and then caring enough to help them perceive their inadequacies.

Moreover, a teacher who adopts this critical approach in teaching can still utilize all the many procedures and strategies presently used for coping with classes or twenty (or thirty or forty!) students. The teacher will, however, approach these strategies differently, using films, filmstrips, teaching machines, and all the instructional technology to present information for students to encounter critically. He or she will not use these techniques to inculcate information the student must accept. The teacher will probably have students take more tests and write more papers, not to grade or judge them, but to elicit their present knowledge; the comments and criticisms of their tests and papers will be educative, not evaluative. The teacher will probably have more classroom discussions. These will take the form of dialogues, not debates or covert lectures, where the students are led by the nose to some predetermined end. The teacher can have more individual and group work which facilitates the education and criticism of students' knowledge.

The critical approach to teaching is not a method of instruction—it is simply an approach. It mandates no specific ways of teaching. It merely suggests that the teacher adopt the role of helpful critic to aid the student in the advancement of his knowledge.

THE IMPROVEMENT OF DISPOSITIONS

At all levels of education—elementary, secondary, and higher—teachers try to teach dispositions, especially moral and aesthetic dispositions. Teachers try to dispose the young toward what is good and what is beautiful.

The closet-cleaner teacher approaches this negatively. As with skills and ideas, so with dispositions: the teacher wants to improve those that exist. And so with dispositions, as with skills and ideas, the closet-cleaner teacher's does not presume to know what is perfect, what is correct. For as we saw with skills and ideas, the closet-cleaner teacher's expertise consists of knowing what is wrong, what is inadequate; hence the pedagogical task is to get students to focus on what is wrong or inadequate and, if possible, eliminate or diminish it. The closet-cleaner teacher employs this same negative approach toward the improvement of dispositions.

The teacher starts by assuming that students do have dispositions: moral dispositions to behave one way or another toward others; aesthetic dispositions to be moved by some phenomena and not by others. Second, the teacher assumes that the students' dispositions are not perfect. They, like all of us, are morally and aesthetically insensitive. We are all unaware of what is morally wrong with some of the ways we behave toward others, unaware of what is aesthetically inadequate with some of the phenomena that move us. The closet-cleaner teacher assumes, third, that the pedagogical task is to help students improve their dispositions, that is, to help them become less morally and aesthetically insensitive. And the final assumption is that the path to improvement is the critical approach, helping students become more aware of what is morally wrong with some of the ways they behave toward others, and more aware of what is aesthetically inadequate with some of the phenomena that move them.

The main task of the closet-cleaner teacher, then, is the sowing of dissatisfaction. Through criticism, the students become dissatisfied with their dispositions and look for different and better ways of behaving toward others and for new and better sources of aesthetic satisfaction.

The educative process here is the same as with the improvement of skills and ideas: the teacher elicits the dispositions the students have, helps them discover how and in what ways they are inadequate, and finally encourages them to refine, alter, or modify the dispositions.

Most of us in our daily behavior, in how we treat others, and in what we praise and condemn as well as what we ignore, do reveal our moral and aesthetic dispositions. Our environment elicits them spontaneously. Yet our daily activities rarely provide us the opportunity to examine critically our dispositions. We tend to identify ourselves with our dispositions: we are what we do; we are what we value. But if we are to improve our moral and our aesthetic dispositions, if we are to become disposed to act differently and to be moved by different things, then we must separate ourselves from our dispositions. Dispositions must be made public so that we can examine them objectively.

To elicit moral dispositions, to make them public, the teacher can use the humanities, including history. Traditionally, educators construed the study of the humanities as the way to civilize the young, the way to make them human. Through the study of the humanities, teachers traditionally sought to initiate the young into a way of life, a culture—a culture that united them to other human beings, introducing them to something shared by those now living, those long dead, and those yet unborn. In the humanities, the young found those moral dispositions worthy of acquisition, or . . . imitation, at least.

But, if we assume that we can always improve our moral dispositions, the teacher will not look to the humanities as the source of moral authority, the repository of ready-made exemplars, suitable for imitation in our daily lives. Instead, the teacher will look to the humanities to supply a counterenvironment to the present moral environment of the students. By presenting students with stories, tales, and poems, or having them read legends, novels, and histories, the teacher helps them see how people behaved at different times and places and under different conditions. Following this presentation or reading, the teacher will invite the students to criticize the actions of the people involved. The students will criticize from their own points of view, so their criticisms will reveal their own dispositions. These student dispositions become the teacher's target: the teacher aims at them, trying to get the students to probe and criticize, to find out what is wrong with their own dispositions.

In this process, the teacher must pay heed to the works of literature used to elicit the criticisms of the students. The teacher must use serious works, avoiding the shallow, simplistic, moralistic tracts that pass for children's literature, lest the students suspect—rightfully so—that the teacher is trying to indoctrinate them.

To allay all suspicions of indoctrination, the teacher can share four assumptions with the students: that all people have moral dispositions; that none has perfect a moral dispositions; that we can improve our moral disposition; that we can do this via the critical approach.

Sharing these assumptions with the students will help them take part in the dialogue and help them to understand what is going on. These assumptions make manifest the notion that human beings are fallible, so that even when we try to do good, evil is inherent in all our dispositions. Sharing these assumptions will also help students to understand how attempts to justify our behavior, rather than criticize it, prevent moral improvement. For, the teacher can point out, we can always come up with some argument to justify our behavior. But attempts to justify merely reinforce existing dispositions, whereas the whole purpose of the dialogue is to improve those dispositions by finding out what is wrong with them and what is wrong with the criticisms of them.

In a dialogue about moral dispositions, the teacher assumes that the students do have moral values or principles, notions of what is right and wrong. The dialogue focuses on the inconsistencies between the student's disposition and his own principles. The thrust of the dialogue is critical, not justificatory. The participants appraise the dispositions by the student's own criteria for what is wrong, bad, or evil. (Older students in senior high school and college can apply the critical approach to the moral codes themselves, in which case the participants will engage in moral philosophy. Here, too, the approach will be critical, not justificatory. The participants will try to discover what is wrong with the code under consideration: the philosophical quest will be a search for criteria of evil, not criteria of good.)

The critical dialogue about moral dispositions makes all who participate more morally sensitive by making them aware of what is morally wrong with some specific disposition. The elimination of those dispositions and the discovery of other, better ones is up to those who possess them. For in adopting the critical, negative approach to the improvement of dispositions, the teacher forswears telling students what they should do, or even helping them decide what they should do. The pedagogical job is solely that of

critic: helping students see what is wrong with specific dispositions.

In the attempts to improve aesthetic dispositions, the closet-
cleaner teacher can use works from the arts and the humanities to
elicit students' present aesthetic dispositions. Presenting them
with a work of art, the teacher will invite them to explain what is
wrong with it. These criticisms reveal the students' own dispositions—what moves them. These become the teacher's target, and
the teacher tries to hit this target by helping them see the aesthetic inadequacies of the phenomena that move them. I have
already described this educative process, and here I will make only
two comments about eliciting student dispositions and criticizing
them.

Unlike the readiness they evince when invited to make moral
criticisms, students often hesitate to make aesthetic criticisms.
Many are more likely to accept the notion that there are final
authorities in the realm of aesthetics. One way the teacher can
disabuse them of this notion is to point out some of the traditions
in the different arts, traditions that reveal how successive artworks
build upon predecessors by overcoming what artists regard as aesthetic inadequacies. History once again reveals man's perennial
quest for improvement, making clear that no artist in any age or
any place has even attained aesthetic perfection. Nor has any cap-
tured the criteria for it; there are no final authorities.

In the attempt to criticize the students' present dispositions,
the teacher might make comparisons with samples of popular or
youth culture, music, films, stories, or whatever is pertinent. The
teacher must take care to prevent such comparisons from becoming generational confrontations over differences in taste. One can
avoid this by making clear that the educational concern is with the
improvement of our aesthetic dispositions, something that can
take place throughout one's entire life and something that leads
to a richer life. The teacher might even adopt the dictum of T. S.
Eliot: "Fine art is the refinement, not the antithesis, of popular
art." Criticism of what moves the students is not a put-down of
popular or youth culture, but an attempt to broaden and deepen
their aesthetic dispositions.

The comparisons should lead to critical dialogue, directed at what is aesthetically inadequate in the works themselves and what is inadequate in the criticisms themselves. Such dialogue helps to develop aesthetic sensitivity. Through it, participants often come to reperceive the works under scrunity, seeing aesthetic qualities where they had perceived none before.

IMPROVING EDUCATION

In this essay I have argued against teachers construing themselved as promoters of learning. My argument is that such a construction converts education into an authoritarian enterprise and thereby inhibits the improvement or advancement of knowledge.

In place of the promotion of learning, I have suggested that educators consciously take on the task of improving knowledge. To do this, they would begin with the assumption that students already possess learning in some gross, unarticulated fashion students have skills, ideas, and dispositions. The teacher's task is to help improve them. One does this by first eliciting some part of this learning and then helping the student to criticize it. The actual refinement and modificatin of his learning in light of unrefuted criticism is up to the student himself. This process is a continual one, so that the teacher will then elicit and help criticize the newly refined knowledge.

I have suggested various ways the teacher might do this. Undoubtedly, there are other ways, but the important point is to have the teacher construe the pedagogical role as that of a closet cleaner, an improver of learning.

A reconstruction of the role of the teacher into that of a closet cleaner will completely change our conceptions of the beginnings and end of the educational process. Traditionally, we have begun the educational process with an uninformed or ignorant student on the one hand, and a body of real or true knowledge, or "learning," on the other. The process consists of the student acquiring that knowledge, or "learning." The process ends with an informed student, one who possesses true knowledge, or real "learning." Once we reconstruct the role of the teacher as a closet cleaner, we begin the educational process with an informed student on the one hand, and a tradition of ideas, skills, and dispositions on the other. The process consists of the critical engagement of the student with that tradition. This leads to a refinement or modification of the student's learning in light of unrefuted criticism. There is no end to the process; the improvement of knowledge need never stop. Education can continue throughout one's life. Formal education merely initiates the young into the process through which we improve our knowledge or learning—the process of criticism.

I do believe that teachers must stop construing themselves as promoters of learning simply because such a construction actually generates most of the educational problems under discussion today.

Thus, perhaps as much as half of the educational problems recognized today spring from the failure of teachers to do what they are supposed to do: they fail to promote learning in all students. We receive many different explanations of why (some) students fail to learn. The most *hopeless* explanations refer to cultural and social changes over which we have no control and which seem to be irreversible: the decline of religion, the disintegration of the family, the influence of mass media, and unsettling demographic changes. The most *controversial* explanations locate the problem in the student: his heredity or his environment—some children cannot learn because they have the wrong genes or live in the wrong kind of neighborhood. The most *radical* explanations find the root causes in the system—the educational system, or sometimes the socioeconomic system, of Western civilization: the system prevents learning because it alienates and victimizes students. The *most frequently heard* explanation for the failure is poor teaching: teachers fail because they possess inadequate, inappropriate, or no skills; they have poor attitudes toward, or expectations of, their students; or they might fail simply because of their class background or their color.

Each of these explanations has some credibility, and all have led to various policies and programs to improve education. Those like Arthur Jensen who find the failure of learning due to heredity, advocate different kinds of education for different racial groups.[13]

Those like James Coleman, who trace the failure to the environment, endorse heterogeneous classrooms and schools; many of his camp support busing as a means of creating mixed schools.[14] Those like Jonathan Kozol, who locate the failure to learn in the very educational system itself, propose new, different, alternative, or free schools, schools that will promote learning.[15] Those like Colin Greer, who root the causes of failure in the economic and social structure of our society, demand that the schools become agents of social reconstruction, instruments to change and reconstruct the society.[16] Finally, those many critics who lay the blame on the teachers insist that the public should hold the teachers accountable for the learning, or lack of it, that students acquire. This has revived an interest in so-called behavioral objectives, determinate and measurable objectives by which the public can grade teachers.[17]

Each one of these proposals for improvement, like the analysis on which each is based, has some credibility, but only because those who accept each one assume that the teacher's task is to promote learning. I maintain that this is a misguided assumption. This is evident when we look at those cases where teachers do successfully promote learning. Here we encounter the remaining problems—the other half—identified by the critics of today's educational scene.

First of all, when teachers do successfully promote learning for some students while failing to do so for others, they divide the school-age population, and ultimately the society itself, into winners and losers, oppressors and oppressed. Thus, attempts to promote learning leads to deep divisions within the society. Of course such divisions may always exist, but the fact that the school creates them lends them a legitimacy, a permanence that feeds the self-righteousness of the winners and the despair of the losers.[18] And there are other unwanted and unanticipated social consequences brought about when teachers successfully promote learning. For example, Paul Goodman claimed that efforts to promote learning result in the processing of students—processing them from people into personnel, ready and willing to man the centralized, bureaucratized, dehumanized institutions of our civilization.[19] This theme is echoed by Ivan Illich and Everett Reimer, who claim that when schools successfully promote learning they convert the young into mindless believers in, and supporters of, a manipulative society.[20] Other critics have pointed out the dire consequences the promotion of learning has on the quality of education itself. Anxious to be successful "learners," students—aided and abetted by teachers anxious to be successful "promoters"—pursue the form of learning, disregarding its substance. That is, they amass grades and averages, points and credits, degrees and diplomas—all marks of "learning." This demeans the intrinsic worth of education and leads, in S. M. Miller's trenchant term, to "credentialism" in the larger society.

So, whether teachers fail or succeed in the promotion of learning, their attempts actually create those educational and social problems that most upset observers of present-day education. But if we abandon the notion that teachers should promote learning, we can eliminate most of our present difficulties.

To construe the teacher's role as that of improving the learning the student already has is to convert education into an optimistic, not a hopeless, enterprise. Forswearing attempts to control and meddle with those things they cannot and should not control, teachers will direct attention away from social and cultural phenomena, away from the biological makeup of their students and their family backgrounds, toward what they can and should change and reform: their own teaching behaviors. They will develop ways to elicit and modes to criticize their students' present knowledge. And they can both elicit and criticize—hence improve—their students' present knowledge, regardless of heredity and environment, and with no regard for their cultural and social backgrounds. This will not circumvent the reasonable demand for teacher accountability, but it will allow us to conceive it historically rather than teleologically. That is, we would expect teachers to maintain records of their students' ideas, skills, and dispositions—records in writing, on tapes, on video—that will reveal the students' progress in time, showing how some of the inadequacies, errors, and mistakes manifest at one time were diminished or eliminated by a later time.

To construe teaching as improving existing learning will probably lead to a reconstruction of the present educational structure:

tests, grades, and standards of achievement, as well as textbooks, timetables, and class organization would all undergo refinement and modification. But such changes would not be radical, sentimental, or romantic; they would follow from the new construction of the role of the teacher.

NOTES

1. J. Mc.V. Hunt, *Intelligence and Experience* (New York: Ronald Press, 1961).

2. J. A. Comenius, *The Great Didactic*, trans. M. W. Keatinge. (London: Adam and Charles Black, 1896).

3. John Dewey, *Experience and Education* (New York: Macmillan, 1938).

4. George Kelly, "Man's Construction of His Alternatives," *Clinical Psychology and Personality*, ed. B. Maher (New York: Wiley, 1969).

5. Carl Rogers, *Freedom to Learn: A View of What Education Might Become* (Columbus, Ohio: Charles E. Merrill, 1969).

6. See N. Postman and C. Weingartner, *Teaching as a Subversive Activity* (New York: Delacorte Press, 1969); see also John C. Holt, *How Children Learn* (New York: Pitman, 1969).

7. See Karl R. Popper, *The Logic of Scientific Discovery* (New York: Basic Books, 1959); *Conjectures and Refutations: The Growth of Scientific Knowledge* (New York: Basic Books, 1972); *Objective Knowledge* (Oxford: Oxford University Press, 1972). See also Thomas Kuhn, *The Structure of Scientific Revolutions* (Chicago: University of Chicago Press, 1962), and Irme Lakatos and Alan Musgrave, eds., *Criticism and the Growth of Knowledge* (Cambridge: Cambridge University Press, 1970).

8. The Darwinian conception of education outlined here is the same as the ecological approach to improving schools that I present in Chapter 5 of this volume. There I suggest that we begin with the school that presently exists and try to find out what's wrong with it, modifying the existing practices, policies, and procedures of the school in light of the unrefuted criticisms of them. Here, in applying this ecological approach to the process of education itself, I suggest we begin with the learning or knowledge the student already has and try to find out what's wrong with it. Thus, we encourage and support him so that he will modify that knowledge in light of the unrefuted criticisms of it.

9. See Henry J. Perkinson, "The Apology of Socrates," *Journal of Educational Thought* (April 1970). See also Robert McClintock, "Toward a Place for Study in a World of Instruction," *Teachers' College Record* (December 1971).

10. See Maria Montessori, *The Montessori Method*, trans. Anne E. George, (New York: Frederick A. Stokes, 1912).

11. See Barbel Inhelder and Jean Piaget, *The Growth of Logical Thinking from Childhood to Adolescence*, trans. Anne Parsons and Stanley Milgrum (New York: Basic Books, 1958).

12. Here, as throughout the chapter, I have adopted and adapted the epistemological theories of Karl Popper. In addition to the references in note 7, see also the "Autobiography of Karl Popper," *The Philosophy of Karl Popper*, ed. Paul A. Schlipp (LaSalle, Ill.: Open Court, 1974).

13. Arthur R. Jensen, "How Much Can We Boost I.Q. and Scholastic Achievement?" *Harvard Educational Review* (February 1969).

14. James S. Coleman, *Equality of Educational Opportunity: Addresses, Essays and Lectures* (New York: Vintage Books, 1972).

15. Jonathan Kozol, *Free Schools* (Boston: Houghton Mifflin, 1972).

16. Colin Greer, *The Great School Legend: A Revisionist Interpretation of American Public Education* (New York: Basic Books, 1972).

17. See, for example, Leon M. Lessinger, *Every Kid a Winner: Accountability in Education* (Worthington, Ohio: C. A. Jones, 1971).

18. See Henry J. Perkinson, *The Imperfect Panacea* (New York: Random House, 1968).

19. Paul Goodman, *People or Personnel: Decentralizing and the Mixed System* (New York: Random House, 1965).

20. Ivan D. Illich, *Deschooling Society* (New York: Harper and Row, 1971), and Everett Reimer, *School Is Dead* (Garden City, N.Y.: Doubleday Anchor Book, 1971).

PART II

On Reforming Schools

CHAPTER 4

Liberalism and Imaginative Educational Reforms *

RONALD M. SWARTZ

... the liberal position is based on courage and confidence, on a preparedness to let change run its course even if we cannot predict where it will lead.

—F. A. Hayek

OVERVIEW OF THE ARGUMENT

The major question this essay attempts to answer is, "How should the imagination of social theorists be both used and checked in the development and implementation of innovative educational reforms?" [1] I will argue that the imagination of educational theorists should not be restricted in any way during the creation stage of theory development. On the other hand, at the time when innovative educational reforms are ready to be im-

---

* This paper is published here for the first time. A version of this paper was read at the annual meeting of the American Educational Studies Association in Memphis, Tennessee, November 1976.

plemented in society, I will suggest that the imagination of educational theorists may lead to dangerous and harmful social practices. Thus, my claim throughout this paper is that some imaginative educational innovations should not be tried in the real world because educational theorists are fallible human beings who should not always be allowed to do as they wish.

EDUCATIONAL REFORM AND THE NEED FOR SKEPTICISM

Before discussing the central issues of this essay, a few general comments about the process of social reform are in order.

First, I think it is desirable to be skeptical and critical of all efforts to change the way we organize our educational institutions. However, skepticism is at its worst when it leads to inaction or the defense of the status quo; the form of skepticism I endorse suggests that it is desirable for social reformers to propose daring solutions to the educational problems that confront us.[2] Skepticism and caution should enter the picture only at the point of implementing and evaluating new educational programs and policies. Later in this paper I will have more to say about how groups of people might check and even stop social reformers from doing harm. Here I merely wish to note that unlike some educational reformers I do not claim to know what is best for my fellow human beings. Although at times I may seem to be dogmatic, this should not be misunderstood: I do not believe I possess the "truth"; my skepticism is founded on the fallibilist notion that truth is an unattainable goal, and I view all intellectual work as potentially fallible.[3]

Although I can be viewed as a skeptic, I think systematic procedures which might enable us to improve our understanding of how best to use our educational institutions can be developed. Unfortunately, my hope for systematic educational experimentation has not yet been realized. Most theories of educational reform are either too radical or too conservative to have a meaningful effect on our understanding of the educational process. Specifically, radical educational theorists often recommend grand utopian schemes for the total revamping of society and its educational systems; the unhappy result of such proposals is often inaction, violent revolutionary activity, or total disillusionment.[4] On the other hand, conservative theorists often attempt to develop educational innovations that are consistent with tradition or with what the public demands; when conservative reforms are used in our schools, very little changes; too, these reforms lack imagination, since reformers do not think daringly but instead try to make their reforms acceptable to public opinion.[5]

Here I will attempt to begin the process of developing a liberal theory of educational reform that competes with both radical and conservative notions about how to change society and its educational institutions. I have chosen to call my ideas about educational experimentation a liberal theory of reform because many of the points I argue for have their historical roots in the works of liberal philosophers and political theorists such as John Stuart Mill, Bertrand Russell, John Dewey, Walter Lippmann, F. A. Hayek, and Karl Popper. Although these theorists have often profoundly disagreed with one another, many of their ideas on social reform will be the basis for the arguments endorsed here.[6]

In short, this essay attempts to explain how a society can develop and implement experimental educational programs. However, rather than giving a comprehensive overview of the many issues associated with social reform, my discussion here will at times raise more problems than it attempts to solve; and a systematic evaluation of the variations of radical and conservative views of reform is beyond the scope of this paper. Nevertheless I should add that I do mean to suggest that the liberal theory of reform I develop may eventually prove to be better than other ideas about how to change and improve our educational institutions.

STAGES OF EXPERIMENTATION; THE SCIENTIFIC IMAGINATION

My approach to educational reform assumes that this process can be divided into at least two distinct steps. First, there is the *creation stage* of theory development during which theorists imagine how they would like the world to be. Second, there is the *implementation stage* of theory development when theorists try to make the world conform with their ideas. During the creation stage, society should allow educational theorists to imagine bold and daring innovations that challenge conventional notions about schooling. However, when deciding on whether to implement new policies, it is sometimes necessary to reject some innovations, since some social experiments could have disastrous effects.

I am suggesting that we need a *continuous critical dialogue* between social theorists and the different groups of people who are interested in educational reform. In this dialogue, educational reformers and their critics would be responsible for trying to weed out those innovations that seem to be dangerous and harmful. Furthermore, reformers would be responsible for trying to explain why their innovations were desirable and worthwhile. Hopefully, the end products of these continuous dialogues would be improved ways to educate people.

At this point, let us briefly review some of the ideas Popper has endorsed about the way in which scientific knowledge grows and develops.[7] Popper's ideas about scientists making bold *conjectures* to solve their problems is incorporated in what I have referred to as the creation stage of theory development, and my suggestion that societies be critical throughout the implementation stage attempts to apply Popper's notions about *refutations* and criticism to the process of educational experimentation. Thus, following Popper, it is possible to claim that our knowledge about education can greatly be improved if we can learn what not to do. The process of improving educational practice and theory often involves weeding out ideas that could have unintended, harmful consequences.[8]

The weeding out of inadequate or harmful theories has to be done only at the implementation stage of reform, not at the creation stage, because theories that are not put into practice cannot cause harm. Thus, it is possible to claim that the role of imagination in the development of a theory is different from the role of imagination in the testing of a theory. Although I would readily admit that it is necessary for scientists to use their imaginations to discover new ways to test ideas, using the imagination for this purpose is obviously quite different from using the imagination to conjecture bold new theories. When imagination is used to develop new kinds of tests for a theory, at some point a scientist usually attempts to manipulate physical reality; in contrast, the use of the imagination to develop a theory may not require any contact with the real world; theoretical scientists can do their work purely by using their minds.[9]

I do not mean to suggest that theoretical scientists should be content with developing beautiful idealistic theories that cannot be tested by experience. Good scientific theories need to be tested in the real world; theoretical scientists who develop ideas that cannot be tested by experience contribute very little to our understanding of the empirical world.

Finally, in regard to the use of imagination in the sciences I do not assume that it is necessary for all imaginative ideas to be original.[10] Scientists and social reformers can be viewed as being imaginative even if they are not original. For example, scientists may use their imaginations to apply already known ideas to new problem situations. The requirement that human imagination should be used only to discover unique and original ideas is unnecessarily restrictive. We can use imagination both for the discovery of new theories and for the novel application of already known ideas.

LIBERALISM AND THOUGHT VERSUS ACTION

The distinction between the two stages of social reform is by now apparent, but to avoid any possible misunderstanding, I will develop this distinction somewhat further, since it is certainly possible to view thought as an activity done in the real world. In suggesting that there is a sharp distinction between thought and action, I mean that that such activities as thinking and writing do not necessarily involve more than one person. Thinking, writing, and reading are obviously activities an individual can do without interacting with others or without being concerned with others' rights. But when we act in the physical world, our actions may involve more than one person; whenever two or more people interact with one another, absolute freedom of action is not always possible, because it is often necessary to consider the social, political, and physical realities of a situation. In regard to the difference

between freedom of thought and freedom of action, John Stuart
Mill once observed:

> it is imperative that human beings should be free to form
> opinions and to express their opinions without reserve. . . . let
> us next examine whether . . . men should be free to act upon
> their opinions—to carry these out in their lives without hin-
> drance. . . . No one pretends that actions should be as free as
> opinions. On the contrary, even opinions lose immunity when
> the circumstances in which they are expressed are such as to
> constitute their expression a positive instigation to some mis-
> chievous act.[11]

Another way to understand the liberal distinction between
thought and action is to realize that pure thought, despite the fact
that it has the potential to guide human action, may at times have
no effect on the world. Contrarily, action—the application of a
thought—necessarily involves some contact with the world; hence
when we act, we have to consider the possible consequences of our
actions. Since the consequences of some actions may be viewed as
illegal, undesirable, and harmful for others, it sometimes becomes
necessary for society to try to prevent individuals from acting in
certain ways. The very real distinction between thought and action is important for educational reform; although social reformers should be allowed to propose any theory they can imagine,
they should not be allowed to implement any idea they consider
to be desirable. It is necessary for all societies to have standards
which help people decide if a suggested educational experiment is
desirable and legal; we should always remember that social reformers, like everyone, are fallible human beings who will at times
develop unsatisfactory, and possibly destructive ideas.

THE FALLIBILITY OF REFORMERS—A CAUTION

My reasons for suggesting that social reformers are fallible individuals are extensive and detailed. However, I will briefly summarize with regard to the fallibility of reformers. First, history shows
that social reformers may have a great capacity for doing harm;

both history and reason tell us that social innovators, however well intentioned they may be, are not necessarily reliable authorities in terms of foreseeing what might happen when their ideas are implemented in society. One lesson we can learn from the kinds of social experiments suggested in George Orwell's *Nineteen Eighty-Four* and Aldous Huxley's *Brave New World* is that reformers may create a world worse than the one that exists. In another sense, the kinds of execrable "social experiments" that were carried out in such societies as Nazi Germany should never be allowed to happen in the real world; needless to say, systematic inhumanity is never permissible in any rational, humane society. In brief, it is foolish, uncritical, irresponsible, and possibly lethal for a society to allow all suggested experiments to be tried on human beings. Second, there is no authority or method for proving that social reformers can be relied on to know what is best for the individuals who live in their society. All attempts to demonstrate that social reformers and their ideas are reliable authorities must lead to some kind of irrational commitment or blind adherence to the authority of those who have been placed in positions of power and responsibility. Although social reformers are not typically evil and malicious, they are fallible and hence can and do make mistakes; even if reformers think their experiments are good, any new experiment may unintentionally harm some individuals.[12]

Since social reformers are fallible human beings, quite naturally society must have standards by which to judge whether educational innovations should be rejected or accepted. It seems only reasonable to have guidelines which disallow certain kinds of activities. What the guidelines are may differ from society to society and change from time to time, but educational reformers should not expect their experiments to be peacefully implemented if their ideas are deemed unsatisfactory by the guidelines a society uses to judge acceptable social behavior.

When new experiments are excluded by the standards applied in a given society, it may be both necessary and desirable for people to consider the possibility of changing these standards. Individuals can try to change the standards for acceptable social experimentation in a number of ways. For example, laws could be enacted either to allow or to disallow certain kinds of social experiments. This was done in the United States with regard to the racial integration of schools and, in some parts of the country, of public facilities. Also, revolutions may at times be necessary. This would certainly be the case if reformers were living in a society like Nazi Germany and they wanted to start an educational program such as Summerhill. Finally, the standards used to decide if an innovation is acceptable may be formal or informal. The standards for judging social experiments may be stated in the laws of the land, or they may not involve legal considerations but simply deal with people's beliefs, expectations, and hopes—the mores of the society as a whole.

Because the standards for judging the acceptability of new social experiments are always somewhat vague, it is possible for an innovation to be legally acceptable but socially undesirable, since people may not desire to participate in the experiment that is recommended. Educational reformers should not be crushed or discouraged when people do not wish to take part in their experiments. Rather than see these setbacks negatively, reformers can make a positive interpretation of the inability to implement innovative educational policies. The following interpretations could be made when an experiment is rejected for implementation: (1) the desirable aspects of an experiment have not yet been sufficiently argued for in a convincing manner, and more work has to be done to make a case for the experiment under consideration; (2) the experiment is not as good as it appeared at first and should be rejected or modified; (3) people in society do not yet know enough about the experiment, and it is necessary to try to create a demand for a suggested innovation; and (4) although the individuals who presently live in one's society may not approve of a new experiment, it may be of value to future generations.

What I am suggesting is that social reformers should attempt to evaluate their experiments critically at all times. Rather than passively accept the public's judgments about their experiments, reformers should continue to develop reforms they believe to be valuable, worthwhile, and interesting. However, whereas a reformer should be highly critical of public opinion, at the point of implementing a program a reformer should not ignore what the public is saying.[13] On the contrary, the public has the potential for becoming one of the most important checks on the educational reforms tried in society. As previously noted, at the implementation stage of a social experiment, reformers should not be allowed to do totally as they please. The kinds of social reformers I am talking about need to live in societies that guarantee individuals absolute freedom of thought in order to be able to function at all, but reformers should not expect all of their ideas to be implemented in society.

PIECEMEAL REFORMS AND PILOT PROGRAMS

I wish now to turn to the importance of using pilot programs to test innovative social policies. This notion implies that social experimentation should be done in a piecemeal fashion.[14] That is, rather than involving the entire population in society in a new social experiment, it seems more reasonable to try experiments involving a limited number of people, for a clearly specified time, and with the aim of solving a limited number of problems. One of the most significant features of piecemeal reforms is that they enable society to control the potential harm of a new social policy in that ideas are first tested by a small group of individuals; if an experiment proves to be desirable, it can always be expanded to include more people.

I would now like to consider a particular educational experiment that has interested me for a number of years. Specifically, an innovative educational idea that is not used by most contemporary schools is the following policy: all school members, students included, should be viewed as fallible authorities who are personally responsible for making decisions about their own school activities and many of the policies that govern one's school. I refer to this as *the policy of personal responsibility;* a school that endorses this policy can be labeled a *self-governing school.*[15] Furthermore, the policy of personal responsibility is a partial answer to the following two questions: (1) Which authorities should be responsible for determining what school members do and learn in school? (2) How can we create educational programs which check and diminish the harm school and societal authorities might do to students and other school members?

Although educational alternatives such as self-governing schools may be considered undesirable by many people, these schools do help us see that social policies are theories or hypotheses that attempt to solve problems.[16] In addition, the discussion about self-govenning schools helps us see that a piecemeal approach to educational reform may change many aspects of an educational program. For example, if a self-governing school were to be created in a public school system, some public schools might do away with such traditional things as a standardized curriculum, grade levels, and teacher-determined school rules. However, in order to make such far-reaching reforms as these, it is not necessary to change all the schools in any society; alternative schools can and do exist in some school systems. In other words, a suggested innovative solution to an educational problem might change many difference aspects of *one unit* in a social system, but there is no need to change *all the units* at one time.[17]

Naturally, educational theorists who are interested in doing piecemeal reforms must decide what aspect of a social system they want to change. If they want to reform a part of an educational system, they might take any one of the following as a reference point for change: the curriculum, a certain aspect of the curriculum such as science education, a classroom, a school within a particular school district, an entire school system within a city or state, or the entire educational system within a country. The point of reference one chooses as the focus for change will of course depend on the problem one is dealing with and on the kind of educational policy one is experimenting with. Nevertheless, reformers should realize that there is generally a great deal of interaction among social systems and institutions within society; total isolation of any pilot program seems to be an unattainable goal. Just as natural scientists cannot always create ideal circumstances for their experiments, social reformers should realize that they will be working in situations where it is impossible to control every variable that might affect one's experiment.[18]

When determining the reference point for a specific innovation, educational reformers must consider such variables as the scope of an experiment and the problem situation which has led to a new educational policy. Also, reformers must be specific about the part of the world they are attempting to change and improve.

Finally, it should be noted that piecemeal reformers may or may not have a utopian vision of an ideal world. However, piecemeal educational reformers who have a utopian vision do not attempt to make their dreams a reality for all people; instead, they attempt to make their dreams a reality for some people. Unlike reformers who try to do too much, piecemeal reformers try to create workable pilot programs which adequately test new ideas.[19] In other words, piecemeal reformers may have a utopian vision, but in no way do they assume that their vision is the true or perfect description of what is best for all people; they recognize their fallibility and they attempt to improve their utopian ideas in the light of experience and criticism.

DANGERS OF REFORM; THE NEED FOR DIVERSITY

The testing of innovative social and educational policies should be viewed somewhat differently from the testing of theories in the natural sciences. Although there are some factors common to all human attempts to understand various aspects of the world, when we deal with educational problems and innovations we have to test our theories on real human beings. It is one thing to say that scientists should test the bold theory, "All the planets orbit the sun," and another thing to say that social reformers should test the theory, "People learn to read best when they are beaten and tortured with a whip." This latter idea can be tested only if some individuals are tortured. As many parents will tell you, "It is all right to use someone else's child for your educational experiments, but don't use my child as one of your guinea pigs."

Those parents who would object to using their children in an educational experiment do make an important point. All educational experimentation involves some risks.[20] However, if we want to improve both the practice of education and our understanding of the educational enterprise, then we must take some chances. Improvement in the way we educate people can come about only if we are willing to change old ideas and experiment with new ones. Unfortunately, there is no way to guarantee that improvement will always be realized by the new ideas reformers develop, but we can help the cause for better schools if we encourage reformers to use their imaginations to come up with creative and innovative educational policies and programs.

In order to improve its educational institutions, a society must allow for some form of social experimentation. Furthermore, for those who favor liberal piecemeal reforms, a society should encourage the creation of diverse and conflicting educational experiments;[21] within the range of socially acceptable limits, reformers should be allowed to try out ideas and programs which compete with one another to solve the same or different educational problems. Nevertheless, a liberal theory of reform does not have to be associated with relativism. For liberals such as Popper, scientific theories and social policies can at times be compared and evaluated. Popper and others have argued that our ideas often compete with one another as a means of solving the same problem; when two or more competing theories attempt to solve the same problem, we may be able to devise empirical tests which enable us to discern that one theory is better than another.

Discussions about how to evaluate competing scientific hypotheses involve sophisticated arguments associated with such topics as probability, verification, refutation, and many other issues of interest to philosophers of science. In this essay I do not want to review different notions about how to test and compare *competing* empirical theories.[22] What I do want to suggest is that a major aspect of a piecemeal approach to educational reform is that it incorporates the liberal arguments related to the toleration of diversity and freedom of thought. Traditionally, liberal political and philosophical theorists have held that a society should allow diverse and conflicting ideas to compete openly with one another.[23] One consequence of such competition is that at any given time many educational revolutions may be going on simultaneously. This notion of *simultaneous revolutions* is compatible with a liberal piecemeal theory of educational reform as long as the different revolutions have been judged to be socially acceptable by the standards used to evaluate educational innovations. Whatever the case, no suggested revolution should ever be considered the final step in the process of educational reform, since all innovations may be improved upon by human ingenuity and imagination.

CONCLUDING REMARKS

We should not be discouraged by the fact that educational reformers are fallible human beings who often make mistakes.[24] Human fallibility should be accepted as a fact of life. What we must do is learn how to avoid disastrous mistakes and use whatever mistakes we make to improve the world we live in. This paper has necessarily barely touched on the subject of bringing about systematic and meaningful social change, but I believe the discussion here can provide a start for a dialogue over various problems related to educational reform. My arguments suggest that we consider questions such as the following: In what ways can educational reform benefit from a scientific approach to problem solving? How can educational reformers best use their imaginations? What kinds of checks and limitations should we place on the development of an innovation and its implementation? How can we decide if an innovation is indeed an improvement over past practices?

Although I have suggested *tentative* solutions to some of the problems that confront educational reformers, neither liberalism nor any other social philosophy can solve all the problems that confront us in creating better social institutions. No doubt, the ideas I have presented will at some time be superseded by others. We can only hope that during this never ending dialogue about how to improve our schools we will occasionally find better and more reasonable ways to deal with our educational problems.

NOTES

1. A version of this paper was read at the November 1976 American Educational Studies Association Convention in Memphis, Tennessee. The epigraph at the beginning of this essay is from F. A. Hayek, *The Constitution of Liberty* (Chicago: University of Chicago Press, 1960), p. 400.

2. Throughout this paper I will rely heavily on the philosophy of science that has been developed by Karl R. Popper. My intent here is to offer an interpreta-

tion of Popper's view of science that can be used in relationship to solving educational problems. For an introduction to some of Popper's major ideas about social reform see the following: Karl R. Popper, *The Poverty of Historicism* (London: Routledge and Kegan Paul, 1963), pp. 55–71; *The Open Society and Its Enemies*, vol. 1 (New York: Harper and Row, 1962), pp. 157–68; *Conjectures and Refutations: The Growth of Scientific Knowledge* (New York: Basic Books, 1962), pp. 336–46.

3. For statements from philosophers who endorse the notion that absolute truth is the goal of inquiry in spite of man's fallibility see the following: Bertrand Russell, *Portraits from Memory* (New York: Simon and Schuster, 1969), pp. 178–84; *A History of Western Philosophy* (New York: Simon and Schuster, 1945), pp. 827–28; Karl R. Popper, *Objective Knowledge* (London: Oxford University Press, 1972), pp. 191–205. Finally, for my early ideas on knowledge being fallible see the following: Ronald Swartz, "Problems and Their Possible Uses in Educational Programs," *Philosophy of Education 1973: Proceedings of the Twenty-ninth Annual Meeting of the Philosophy of Education Society*, ed. Brian Crittenden (Edwardsville, Ill.: Philosophy of Education Society, 1973), pp. 135–45; "Induction as an Obstacle for the Improvement of Human Knowledge," *Philosophy of Education 1974: Proceedings of the Thirtieth Annual Meeting of the Philosophy of Education Society*, ed. Michael J. Parsons (Edwardsville, Ill.: Philosophy of Education Society, 1974), pp. 375–87; chapter 2 of this volume.

4. An example of a contemporary educator who opts for utopian educational and social reforms is Ivan Illich. For one of his many statements about how to revamp society totally see Ivan Illich, *Deschooling Society* (New York: Harper and Row, 1971). Although it is possible to agree with much of Illich's criticism of the educational systems in Western societies, one should be leery of his radical utopian plans which may lead nowhere. For a discussion about some of the dangers associated with Illich's utopianism see Neil Postman, "My Ivan Illich Problem," *After Deschooling What*, ed. Alan Gartner, Collin Greer, and Frank Riessman (New York: Harper and Row, 1973), pp. 137–47.

5. An example of a contemporary educational reform movement that attempted to answer "public opinion" is the curriculum movement of the 1960s which favored the teaching of the "structure of knowledge" in our schools. For references that explain how the structure of knowledge movement answered and served public opinion see Robert E. Mason, *Contemporary Educational Theory* (New York: David McKay, 1972), pp. 136–75; Harry S. Broudy, *The Real World of the Public Schools* (New York: Harcourt Brace Jovanovich, Inc., 1972), pp. 23–28. It is important to note here that advocates of the teaching of the structure of knowledge may not have consciously known that their reforms were an answer to public demands, but my claim here is that all educational reformers should try to develop their ideas without regard for public opinion. For a statement about the dangers of relying on public opinion see the following: Walter Lippmann, *The Public Philosophy* (Boston: Little, Brown, 1955), pp. 16–27; Popper, *Conjectures and Refutations*, pp. 347–54.

6. Those who are part of the liberal tradition have often been highly critical of the central ideas associated with a liberal philosophy. For statements by liberals who have been critical of their own intellectual tradition see the following: John Dewey, *Liberalism and Social Action* (New York: Capricorn Books, 1935), pp. 28-55; Walter Lippmann, *The Good Society* (Boston: Little, Brown, 1937), pp. 183-240; Hayek, *The Constitution of Liberty*, pp. 706-11; Popper, *Conjectures and Refutations*, pp. 347-54; Bertrand Russell, *Power* (New York: W. W. Norton, 1938), pp. 214-19.

7. See the references in notes 2 and 3. Also, it should be noted here that throughout this essay I assume that in many ways there are similarities between scientific inquiry and the process of attempting to understand educational problems. Of course, there is nothing new about trying to take a scientific approach to the study of social situations. People familiar with the work of John Dewey will find this idea old hat. For one of Dewey's many statements about the unity of method in the natural and social sciences see John Dewey, *Logic: The Theory of Inquiry* (New York: Holt, Rinehart and Winston, 1938), p. 101. Although Dewey and others have endorsed the notion of a unity of method in the sciences, this notion has often incorporated the idea that the scientific method relied heavily on inductive procedures. For one of Dewey's many statements about the importance of induction in a method of inquiry see John Dewey, *How We Think* (Chicago: Henry Regnery, 1933), pp. 173-74. In contrast to Dewey's inductivist views, Popper has tried to offer an interpretation of the scientific method that does not rely on inductive procedures. For one of Popper's many statements about the need to offer a noninductivist view of the scientific method see Karl R. Popper, *The Logic of Scientific Discovery* (New York: Harper and Row, 1959), pp. 27-34. Finally, the similarities between Dewey's and Popper's ideas have been discussed in D. C. Phillips, "Popper and Pragmatism: A Fantasy," *Educational Theory* 25, no. 1 (Winter 1975): 83-91. In his essay Phillips argues that Popper's ideas on the scientific method are very similar to Dewey's. As I see matters, Phillips is mistaken to emphasize the similarities between Popper's and Dewey's views; much can be gained by evaluating the different views these philosophers have on the role of induction in science.

For essays that attempt to make a distinction between Popper's ideas and those of others such as the pragmatists see the following: Joseph Agassi, "The Novelty of Popper's Philosophy of Science," *International Philosophical Quarterly* 8, no. 3 (September 1968): 442-63; Swartz, "Induction as an Obstacle for the Improvement of Human Knowledge," pp. 375-87; chapter 2 of this volume.

8. For introductory comments about the importance of studying the unintended consequences of social policies see the following: F. A. Hayek, *Studies in Philosophy, Politics and Economics* (New York: Simon and Schuster, 1969), pp. 96-105; Popper, *The Open Society and Its Enemies*, vol. 2, p. 93, and *Conjectures and Refutations*, pp. 123-124.

9. An excellent discussion on how theoretical scientists can have "idealized experiments" can be found in the following: Albert Einstein and Leopold Infeld,

The Evolution of Physics (New York: Simon and Schuster, 1967), pp. 6-7; Leopold Infeld, *Albert Einstein* (New York: Charles Scribner's Sons, 1950), pp. 46-55.

10. For a discussion on how people can be imaginative about already known ideas see the following: Hayek, *The Constitution of Liberty*, pp. 1-2; Agassi, "The Novelty of Popper's Philosophy of Science," pp. 442-63.

11. John Stuart Mill, *On Liberty* (Baltimore: Penguin Books, 1974), p. 119. For more recent statements about the liberal distinction between freedom of thought and freedom of action see the following: Bertrand Russell, *Skeptical Essays* (New York: Barnes and Noble, 1963), pp. 125-38; Hayek, *The Constitution of Liberty*, pp. 11-17.

12. See the references in notes 3 and 8. Also, for further information about the arguments related to viewing all scientists and their ideas as fallible authorities see the following: Charles Sanders Peirce, "The Scientific Attitude and Fallibilism," *Philosophical Writings of Peirce*, ed. Justus Buchler (New York: Dover Publications, 1955), pp. 42-59, and Popper, *Conjectures and Refutations*, pp. 3-30. It is important to emphasize here that the criticisms of authority have been known for a long time, but they have not been systematically incorporated into theories about the scientific study of educational problems.

13. See the last two references in note 5.

14. For statements about piecemeal social reforms see the following: Popper, *The Open Society and Its Enemies*, vol. 1, pp. 158-68, and *The Poverty of Historicism*, pp. 64-70. Also, the notions associated with a theory of piecemeal reforms seem to be endorsed by F. A. Hayek. For a good overview of Hayek's views on social experimentation see Hayek, *The Constitution of Liberty*, pp. 39-53. Finally, it should be noted that Dewey also seemed to advocate some form of piecemeal reforms in John Dewey, "Progressive Education and the Science of Education," *Dewey on Education*, ed. Martin S. Dworkin (New York: Teachers College Press, 1959), pp. 113-26. In this essay Dewey argues that progressive educational reforms may not succeed, and he recommends that progressive educators use "candor and sincerity to keep track of failures as well as successes." (p. 126). For references that explain how Dewey's view of science is different from Popper's see note 7.

15. My early ideas about the policy of personal responsibility and self-governing schools can be found in the following: Ronald Swartz, "Education as Entertainment and Irresponsibility in the Classroom," *Science Education*, 58, no. 1 (January-March 1974): pp. 119-25; "Some Criticisms of the Distribution of Authority in the Classroom," *Focus on Learning* 4, no. 1 (Spring-Summer 1974): 33-40; "Schooling and Responsibility," *Science Education* 59, no. 3, (July-September 1975): pp. 409-12; chapter 9 of this volume. In addition, for an explanation of the sense in which I view the policy of personal responsibility as an innovative and imaginative idea see Joseph Agassi, "The Novelty of Popper's Philosophy of Science," pp. 442-63.

16. For discussions about how social policies are attempts to solve problems

see the following: Karl R. Popper, *The Open Society and Its Enemies*, vol. 1, pp. 157-68; I. C. Jarvie, *The Revolution in Anthropology* (Chicago: Henry Regnery, 1964), pp. xiii-xvi; F. A. Hayek, *The Counter Revolution of Science* (London: Collier-Macmillan Ltd., 1955), pp. 13-16. Also see the references in notes 3, 7, and 15.

17. For an example of an advocate of piecemeal reforms who recommends that social theorists set priorities on the problems solved by an educational experiment see Joseph Agassi, "The Preaching of John Holt," *Interchange* 1, no. 4 (1970): 115-18. Also, for a historical account of how schools often do not set priorities on the problems they attempt to solve see Henry J. Perkinson, *The Imperfect Panacea: American Faith in Education, 1865-1965* (New York: Random House, 1968). Finally, for an account of how I view a school and a society's educational institutions as social systems see Popper, *The Poverty of Historicism*, pp. 65-67.

18. See the references in notes 2, 3, 12, and 14.

19. Refer to notes 2, 4, and 17.

20. Refer to notes 2, 8, and 14.

21. For discussions about the need for scientific communities to encourage the development of competing and conflicting theories see the following: Joseph Agassi, "The Nature of Scientific Problems and Their Roots in Metaphysics," *The Critical Approach to Science and Philosophy*, ed. Mario Bunge (London: Collier-Macmillan Ltd., 1964), pp. 189-211; P. K. Feyerabend, "How to Be a Good Empiricist—A Plea for Tolerance in Matters Epistemological," *The Philosophy of Science*, ed. P. H. Nidditch (Glasgow: Oxford University Press, 1968), pp. 12-39; Jarvie, *The Revolution in Anthropology*, pp. 7-15; Popper, *Conjectures and Refutations*, pp. 66-96.

22. See the references in notes 2, 3, and 21.

23. Refer to notes 11, 16, 17, and 21.

24. A detailed account of how I view the process of learning from mistakes can be found in chapter 2 of this volume.

CHAPTER 5

How to Improve Your School*

HENRY J. PERKINSON

Most writers on this topic make much more modest claims; *they* title *their* books and articles, "How to Change Your Schools" or "How to Innovate." They do not explicitly promise that the suggested changes or innovations will necessarily "improve" your school. Yet, the promise is implicit, isn't it? Otherwise, why change? Why innovate? Actually, I don't think these other writers are modest at all. They are cautious . . . because they have a defective theory of improvement. So, rather than bare their theory of improvement to questions about its validity and reliability by talking about how to improve schools, they immunize their theory of improvement to critical questions by talking instead about the more neutral enterprise of how to "change" your school.

To see that most educational reformers have concealed (and defective) theories of improvement, we need only follow the typical career pattern of the most recent. Sooner or later, most who set about to reform the schools begin by talking and writing about

---

* This paper is published here for the first time. A version of this paper was read at the annual meeting of the American Educational Studies Association in Memphis, Tennessee, November 1976.

the matter of resistance to change.[1] Not only do they spend a great deal of energy devising ways of dealing with resistance to change, but in time, many who actually try to reform the schools decide that it is impossible to improve the actual ongoing educational instutions: *there is too much resistance to change.* Those—now chastened—reformers who continue to hope for improvement in education often move into the free schools, or the alternative school movement.[2]

Some of those who go into the alternative school movement hope that the alternative schools may turn out to be bellwethers for the establishment schools. But others in the movement—the more disenchanted—merely await the total collapse of the unchanging and unchangeable establishment schools.

What we have, then, is a great deal of evidence that attempts at educational improvement of the ongoing education institutions always meet resistance, and some dramatic evidence that the resistance is often powerful enough to prevent any improvement at all. A dismal state of affairs, indeed.

Yet, rather than follow these would-be reformers in citing resistance to change as the cause of failure, I find it just as plausible to suppose that most school reforms fail because they have a defective theory of improvement.

THE TELEOLOGICAL APPROACH TO IMPROVEMENT

Most current theories of educational improvement are teleological. A teleological theory of improvement insists that we start off with an end, a goal, an ideal, or ideal criteria for a good school—and then try to move a real school, an existing school, toward that ideal, or toward those goals or criteria.

The trouble with a teleological approach to improvement is that it ignores human fallibility. Now, most reformers, even school reformers, will accept the proposition that human beings are fallible. So they have no trouble agreeing that the schools we have created are not perfect. Most will go further to agree that we can never create perfect schools, that we are doomed to having imperfect educational institutions. But, of course, we are even worse off than that: we cannot even *imagine* or *dream up* a perfect school.

And if by chance, as it were, we did dream up a perfect school, we would not recognize it as such, since we are not omniscient.

Yet many reformers will reply that yes, fallible human beings cannot create, discern, or concoct perfect aims or ideals; but they insist that reformers can come up with goals or aims that are better than those in vogue. But the reply to this is that even if reformers do come up with better aims and goals, they still face another dimension of human fallibility: human beings are neither omnicompetent nor omnipotent. So when reformers try to move the school toward those "better" goals or aims, there will be unintended, unexpected, and unwanted consequences—consequences that adversely affect others: students, teachers, administrators, and parents, for example. Moreover, since we are not omniscient (as well as neither omnicompetent nor omnipotent), the reformers will often fail to perceive those unanticipated adverse consequences.

It is important to note that I am not arguing against teleology. I think that people, and institutions, too, have goals and aims and ends. These goals help individuals and institutions guide and direct their actions and behavior. I am only arguing against employing a teleological approach to improvement. The goals and aims of an institution—such as a school—are irrelevant to its improvement, just as the goals and aims of an individual are irrelevant to his actual improvement. I have argued that because we are fallible we cannot come up with a perfect goal or aim, and second that the actions we set afoot to attain any aim will have adversive consequences that we can neither predict nor control. So it is not the purpose, aim, or goal of an action, a policy, or a procedure that determine whether it was bad, but its actual consequences.

These arguments point to an alternative to the teleological approach to improvement, for if we can eliminate or diminish the adverse consequences of the actual behavior, we will improve it. If in a school, for example, we modify our present practices, policies, or procedures, and thereby do eliminate or reduce their adverse consequences, then we will have improved them. I call this an ecological approach to improvement.

THE ECOLOGICAL APPROACH TO IMPROVEMENT

We have only begun to apply the ecological approach to industry in our search for better solutions to our problems of production. In recent years, critics have heightened our consciousness of the adverse consequences of many of the present modes of production. These critics have made us aware that past (teleological) efforts to improve production have often resulted in the exploitation of the environment and the manipulation and victimization of people. They call for an ecological approach to improvement. This consists of the modification of present arrangements in light of their adverse consequences on the environment.

There are three assumptions inherent in an ecological approach to improvement. First, one assumes that whatever is to be improved—in this case, a school—is part of interconnected networks of other phenomena (ecosystems), as well as being itself made up of numerous interconnected networks (ecosystems). Thus, every practice of a school, every procedure, and every policy has manifold consequences throughout the ecosystem of the school and the ecosystems of which it is a part.

The second assumption is that we fallible beings cannot fully comprehend those multiple and variegated networks that make up the school, nor those of which the school is a part. This means that we can never grasp all the consequences of our policies, practices, and procedures. Put simply, it means we never know what we are doing. However, we can, if we try, detect *some* of the consequences of the existing policies, practices, and procedures. And the consequences of most interest to those concerned with improvement are the unanticipated consequences, the unwanted ones, those that adversely affect other elements of the systems networks. If we can modify the existing arrangements of the school in light of their adverse consequences, then we will have improved the school.

But—and this is the third assumption of an ecological approach to improvement—no one person or group can ever perceive all the adverse consequences of the present arrangements. So we not only

never know what we are doing, we never even know how much bad
we are doing. This is why we need critics.

The essence of the ecological approach to improvement is criticism—criticism of present and proposed arrangements from as
many different points of view as possible, from all elements of the
systems networks. Only through criticism can we discover the actual adverse consequences, so that we may modify what exists or
what is being proposed.

ADVANTAGES AND LIMITATIONS OF AN
ECOLOGICAL APPROACH

The primary advantage of an ecological approach to improvement is that it is in keeping with the human condition of
fallibility. Thus, would-be reformers do not have to assume omniscience about the aims or goals of a school. (This avoids endless
arguments.) With the ecological approach, the would-be reformer
begins with an existing school that has policies and procedures.
The task of improvement is twofold: first, to discover the actual
bad consequences of the existing policies and procedures—the adverse consequences to the elements of the systems networks; second, to modify or reform those existing policies and practices in
such a way that those adverse consequences are eliminated or diminished. Nor need the ecological reformer presume omniscience
about the consequences of the existing arrangements. Those people who actually experience adverse consequences are the ones
who will identify them as such.

A related advantage of the ecological approach is that it forces
would-be reformers from presuming omnicompetence or omnipo-
tence. Unlike the teleological reformer, the ecological reformer
avoids the obsessive, and fruitless, quest for power and control
over all the elements of a school. The ecological approach instead
summons would-be reformers to the more practicable task of cir-
cumscribing the existing power in the school, the task of making
those who exercise power accountable to all who are affected by
their decisions.

As to the limitations of an ecological approach to improving
schools, the first one to note is that it does not produce a good

school. If we take our fallibility seriously, we will forswear any attempts to do this. With the ecological approach, we limit ourselves to to terms "bad" and "better." A bad school is one that people complain about; a better school is one where evils specifically complained about have been eliminated or diminished. So we simply hope to produce a better school, but we have no way of knowing whether or not improvement actually takes place except through history: comparing the present with the past in order to ascertain that the concrete evils identified in the past have been eliminated.

(A similar limitation applies to the ecological approach itself. That is, we cannot say that this is a good approach. We can only make the more modest claim that it is a better approach than a teleological approach, since it is more consonant with our human fallibility.)

Another limitation of the ecological approach is that it is not an approach to decision making. It does not tell how to make better decisions. All it can do is help to improve decisions already made—by having all affected by a decision criticize it. I would also note here that since those who make a decision are not usually inclined to be critical of it, the ecological approach does not advocate participatory decision making. The way to improve decisions is not to have all affected by the decision participate in the making of it—for they can make mistakes, too—but rather to insure that all affected by a decision are free to criticize it. This means that all must have access to, and can secure a response from, the decision makers.

The ecological approach, therefore, does not seek to do away with the existing decision-making authorities in the school. Teachers and administrators will continue to make most of the decisions about what goes on in the school. But it does aim to eliminate authoritarianism. In an authoritarian school, the decision makers brook no criticism of their decisions; they act with impunity, accountable to no one for the policies they promote, the procedures they employ, the practices they engage in.

One other limitation to the ecological approach: it does not assign guilt or innocence. It pays no heed to intentions or motives, only to consequences. Ecological reformers do not play the blame game; they seek to indict no one. The object of the ecological approach is to find out what is wrong, not who is wrong. In eschewing the blame game, ecological reformers can simply acknowledge that those who make decisions in the schools are fallible. So those who adopt the ecological approach can admit that the inadequate, stupid, even evil policies and practices found in schools are the result of human action, but not of human design. Rather than credit these policies and practices to the wicked motives of evil men, they can credit them to the ignorance of fallible human beings.

THE LURE OF THE TELEOLOGICAL APPROACH

Throughout most of Western history, we have been under the spell of the teleological approach to improvement. That spell is broad and deep. It springs from the difficulty we all have in accepting our fallibility. We strive to transcend the human condition and become like gods. (Hence, the greatest human sin is pride, or hubris.)

We all want to be like the Divine Creator of the Bible who, you recall, "created all things and they were good." Man is a creator of sorts, but what he creates is never perfect, never good. And this we have difficulty accepting: we try to ignore the fact that all we create is in some way very inadequate. (Hence, we usually seek to justify what we have created; try to *prove* that it is good.)

There is another way we try to become like the Divine Creator of the Bible. Like him, we attempt to create *ex nihilo*—out of nothing. Thus, we try to create good schools out of the ideas or ideals of a good school. But since ideal schools do not exist, this is simply an attempt to create out of nothing.

I have speculated that we are lured to the teleological approach to improvement because we have difficulty in accepting our human condition of fallibility and strive to be like gods. The ecological approach, however, does allow us to construe ourselves as creators—fallible creators. This means that whatever we create (e.g., schools) can always be improved. So, unlike the biblical Creator who completed his task of creation in six days, human beings are continual creators—they can always improve what they have already created. And instead of creating out of nothing, fallible human beings create, or improve, by modifying what already exists, what they have already created (e.g., schools). The source of human creativity, or improvement, is the recognition that what exists (e.g., schools) is in some way inadequate—and needs modification.

An ecological approach to improving schools is a process of continual criticism of existing policies, practices, and procedures. For it to work, three guarantees are necessary. First, all those adversely affected by the existing arrangements should have access to the decision makers to voice their criticisms. Second, all criticisms should lead to critical dialogue between the critics and the decision makers. Third, all unrefuted criticisms should lead to some modification of the existing arrangements in order to eliminate or diminish the evil complained about. Let me now make some suggestions about how we can supply these guarantees.

GUARANTEEING ACCESS TO DECISION MAKERS

If we can cast off the spell of the teleological approach to improvement, we can begin to employ the ecological approach. Yet, we have only to contemplate employing such an approach to come to realize the barriers to it inherent in most schools. Most schools are not institutions that promote, let alone encourage, criticism of the arrangements within. Teachers rarely (openly) criticize the decisions of school administrators; pupils rarely (openly) criticize teachers' decisions. Moreover, if such criticism emerges, there is a tendency among schoolmen to view it as insubordination, as insolent or disruptive behavior. Rarely is it construed as the initial move in the process of improvement of the school.

So even if you shake loose from the hold of the teleological approach and want to try the ecological approach to improving your school, you run smack into a closed system. But there are some ways to combat it.

The best place to begin is with yourself. You, whether a teacher or an administrator, do have some decision-making powers that affect the lives of others in the school. By beginning with those arrangements over which *you* have control, you can more easily initiate the expression of criticism—the first phase of the ecological approach.

Look as critically as you can at what you are doing—concentrating on those things you could do differently.

If you are a teacher, it might be such seemingly minor matters as seating arrangements in the class, or such serious matters as the way you assign final grades, or the choice of textbooks or collateral reading, or homework assignments, or the way you manage any of the myriad of administrative details in the classroom. Or the way you teach arithmetic, the number of tests you give, the clarity of your explanations of the material, or any matter related to your instructional practices. If you are an administrator, look as critically as you can at the various decisions you have made that determine policies, practices, and procedures in your school or department.

You will—unless you are totally dogmatic (in which case you won't have read this far)—find at least one policy, practice, or procedure that merits change. But don't change it. You are not a perfect critic. You might be wrong. Instead, present the matter to those affected by it—to the teachers, or to the students—and ask them to criticize it, ask them to tell you what's wrong with it. It is important to start off with a specific item for criticism; otherwise you will merely precipitate a general groan-and-gripe session. It is also important to start off with an item you are not strongly committed to—something you could easily change. A third warning: don't ask them to tell you what to do. You should not abrogate your decision-making authority, although you can entertain their suggestions. The focus, however, should be on the inadequacy, impracticality, or irrelevance of the specific policy, practice, or procedure—or of the harm or injustice it perpetuates. You should try to get the critics to make their criticisms as specific as possible.

At the end of such a session—what I will call a critical dialogue— after discussing one or more existing arrangements, you might ask those present to suggest other items for future critical dialogues. You can arrange to hold these dialogues at regular intervals with an announced agenda so that all involved will be prepared to participate.

In addition to regularly scheduled meetings to criticize the existing arrangements, you can also make provisions to handle special matters—particular decisions that adversely affect one or more people. You could do this by means of criticism boxes (instead of suggestion boxes) and specially set aside class time, after-class time, or office time. Where all adversely affected have access to you, an ad hoc critical dialogue in class or office may suffice to redress the wrong, or it may require an extraordinary meeting with all the students or all the teachers involved. You will need regularized procedures for convening such meetings—procedures known to all.

In addition to providing access for all affected to criticize the existing arrangements you have control over, you can also furnish them the opportunity to criticize proposed changes in the arrangements, especially when those proposed changes will be difficult to undo once carried out. I have in mind such proposed changes as: class reorganization, textbook adoption, and major curriculum changes. You can set up hearings or periods of consultation on these kinds of proposed changes, placing before those to be affected one or more proposals for them to criticize. Here, it may sometimes be more feasible to consult an advisory group, duly representing *all* affected by a proposed change.

In addition to instituting meetings and hearings devoted to the criticism of existing and proposed arrangements, you can further combat a closed school by striving to make public all your policies, practices, and procedures. Unless people are aware of them, they will be unable to criticize them—unable to protect themselves. One suggestion is to supply periodic reports of your activities, as well as issuing, where possible, written descriptions of established policies and procedures.

Another way to combat a closed school is to agree that all have the right to appeal any decision you make, when critical dialogue does not redress the wrong complained of. This appeal is nothing more than a request for a continuation of the critical dialogue at another, higher level of the school hierarchy. To make this work, you will have to build the necessary safeguards into it so that all who appeal may do so with impunity.

When you begin with yourself and open up your decisions to criticism, you will be apprised of the inadequacies or unfairness of many arrangements over which you have no control. But this provides the opportunity for extending your attempts to combat a closed school. Now you can confront the next higher level of the school hierarchy to initiate the same open conditions for yourself and for those similarly situated as you are trying to create for the people below you. Here it is best to seek out and enlist the support of other, like-minded people who also want to improve the school. Together you can request the decision-making authorities to make public all the policies, practices, and procedures that affect your professional activities. At the same time, you can begin working to make all those in decision-making positions accessible to criticism through means of meetings and hearings—formal and informal—devoted to critical dialogues about existing and proposed arrangements.

CONVERTING CRITICISM TO CRITICAL DIALOGUE

Once you begin to get decision makers—yourself included—more accessible to critics and more open to criticism, you lay bare another set of problems: the reaction to criticism.

Most of us are annoyed by criticism; some of us are taken aback; some are infuriated. When so confronted, we often fall back on tactics to avoid, mute, or squelch it. The two main strategems are cooling the critic and self-justification.

There are various methods of cooling the critic. One is a direct attack, labeling him a malcontent, a chronic complainer—someone whose criticism merits no serious consideration. A variation on this dismisses the critic as someone who lacks legitimacy because he is not an expert, or because he possesses no appropriate credentials; hence, his criticisms are irrelevant because they are based on expectations of the school different from the rest of us (who, of course, are reasonable human beings).

Undoubtedly, you can supply other methods of cooling the critic. The basic strategy consists of preventing anyone from taking the criticism seriously. Once people construe the criticism as unworthy of a rejoinder, nobody will respond to it. Cooling the critic prohibits dialogue.

Sometimes we combine the strategy of cooling the critic with that of self-justification. Here we also ignore the criticism of what exists and turn instead to explaining why what exists is good. This gets us into the process of self-justification—supplying a sanction that all will accept.

Both cooling the critic and self-justification are logically invalid moves. The former always consists of some variation of *argument ad hominem*. The latter always leads to an infinite regress. But logical validity aside, the pity of these stratagems is that through them people seek to immunize existing arrangements against any criticism, thereby preventing any improvement.

Now, it is easy to say that we all should avoid these stratagems and take all criticism seriously, engaging the critics in critical dialogue—easy to say but hard to carry out. But there are some things we can do to encourage critical dialogue.

First of all, we can urge all critics to present their criticisms in an invitational mode. For example, a critic might say something like this: "These are my criticisms. I may, of course, be wrong. If I am, I hope you will help me by pointing out my errors. Still, the arrangements in this school cannot be perfect, can they? So my criticisms may be on the mark and may help us to improve the school."

This invitational mode of criticizing helps to remind those in positions of authority that the present arrangements that hold in the school cannot be perfect, since they were created by fallible men. And the very act of pointing out that the school cannot be perfect holds forth the possibility that it can be improved through criticism. But, at the same time, the invitational mode makes clear that the critics concede that their criticisms could be mistaken, could be in error.

The invitational mode also makes manifest the critic's clear concern with improving, not destroying, the school, and invites those in positions of authority to join him in a mutual quest.

Finally, the invitational mode helps to encourage an acceptance of pluralism, an acceptance of the notion that different people do have different expectations of the school; expectations that all must take seriously. This follows from the admission of human fallibility, since such an admission rules out the presumption that any one expectation or set of expectations—including your own—is the correct, or right one.

Once someone is reminded of his fallibility and the necessary imperfection of all that human beings create (e.g., schools), he is less inclined to try to justify what exists in the school, more open to consider criticism seriously, more ready to engage in critical dialogue.

Another way to foster critical dialogue is to make clear just what a critical dialogue is. A critical dialogue is not a fight nor a game nor a debate. The object is not to win, to prove oneself right. The object is to improve, and to do this we must test, probe, and criticize in order to learn what is wrong. In essence, then, a critical dialogue is an attempt to discover what is wrong—what is wrong with specific policies, practices, or procedures *and* what is wrong with the criticisms of them. For dialogue to take place, you must take one another's criticisms seriously. To do this means to adopt—for purposes of criticism—the other's point of view. So if someone criticizes a decision you have made, an action you have taken, you must, if dialogue is to take place, adopt his point of view in order to criticize his criticism. You have to show him that his criticism is unfounded or based on erroneous assumptions, or some misinterpretation, or lack of understanding, or false knowledge. Often this involves empirical investigation and evidence, at which point you should suspend the dialogue until the evidence is gathered.

If you refute his criticisms satisfactorily—which means that he will be unable to prove you are wrong—then the dialogue ends. If not, he counters with criticisms of your criticisms, to which you respond with criticisms of your own. The dialogue ends when you or your critic is unable to refute the other's criticism. To repeat once more, the upshot of a critical dialogue is improvement in knowledge: you know what's wrong with the existing arrangements, *or* you know what's wrong with some of the criticisms of those arrangements.

Understanding what a critical dialogue is helps us to avoid attempts to cool the critic. We see it is unnecessary to prejudge critics or criticism—labeling them irresponsible or irrelevant. For the critical dialogue itself is the way to sort this out: bad criticism gets refuted. Therefore, *anyone* can participate in the dialogue, but *everyone* has to agree to submit his criticisms to countercriticisms.

Understanding what a critical dialogue is also helps us to see *it* is the best safeguard against the self-indulgent and egoist critic—the chronic complainer. Through the dialogue he encounters the criticisms of others, coming thereby to realize that there is a world full of other people and other points of view, a world he must live in, and with, if the school is to survive and improve.

THE MODIFICATION OF EXISTING ARRANGEMENTS

Even if you can disengage yourself from the teleological approach to improvement and adopt an ecological approach, even if you can reduce the scope of the closed system within your school so that more people can express criticisms, even if you engender response to that criticism in the form of a critical dialogue—even if you do all this, you still confront difficult practical problems when you turn to modify what exists in light of the unrefuted criticisms.

One problem emerges from the fact that we are naturally problem solvers: we are oriented toward finding solutions and answers to whatever problems we encounter. But, being fallible, our solutions and answers are never perfect, never completely adquate. Not being omniscient, any change we or others make in the school will generate a multitude of unanticipated consequences, some of them harmful or undesirable.

Rather than try to transcend our fallible condition, we can try to incorporate it into this practical phase of making changes. One way to do this is consciously to regard each particular modification, refinement, or replacement as an experiment—as a probe, a test, a trial, that will, in time—and with further criticisms—reveal its own inadequacies. To do this is to construct all the arrangements in the school as experiments and to construe improvers as problem raisers, continually trying to improve the school through the continued elimination of errors and inadequacies.

If this experimental stance is adopted, it is advisable to establish a specific trial period for each modification or change of an existing policy, practice, or procedure—stipulating that at the end of the specified time the new arrangements will be open to criticism on the basis of experience with them. Then, after making the refinments needed in light of the unrefuted criticism brought forth at the end of the trial period, we can stipulate a new trial period for the *new* arrangements.

Another kind of practical problem stems from opposition to the proposed modification of what exists. Any change in the existing arrangements may, consequently, adversely affect others. So they will complain and object. Moreover, any change in the existing arrangements may only reduce or diminish the evil complained of, and not eliminate it entirely. So those who suffer most from that evil will complain and object. One group will complain that the proposed modifications go too far; the other, that they do not go far enough.

What affects this issue most is the tolerance level of all involved: How much discomfiture or suffering will they agree to endure? Some understanding of how improvement takes place through the critical approach can help to raise the tolerance level of all. First, all involved should understand that improvement takes place through the eradication of concrete existing evils. Therefore, in making actual modifications of the existing arrangements, we should deal directly with the existing evil specifically identified: eliminate or diminish *it*. Of course, we should try to create arrangements that do minimize *anticipated* evils. But these anticipated evils cannot be taken as reasons for avoiding the diminution of the *existing* evils identified through the critical dialogue.

Second, all involved should understand that improvement is continual. People are less likely to worry about *anticipated* evils once they find that we construe all arrangements as experiments, always open to criticism and revision in light of unrefuted criticism. So people will be less inclined to cry before they are hurt. Protected through the institutional ecological approach, they will be more willing to wait until they have evidence of concrete wrongs before raising their criticisms.

Third, all involved should understand that the ecological approach provides only piecemeal improvement. It rules out sweeping, large-scale changes or experiments, simply because all changes we introduce will have harmful, unintended consequences—large-scale, sweeping changes will precipitate large-scale, sweeping *harmful* consequences. Understanding this helps raise the tolerance level of those who complain about existing evils: they are more likely to accept a diminution of the evil complained of—piecemeal improvement—rather than demand its total elimination, because they recognize that future improvement is always possible. They know they can always, later, again raise their criticisms and secure further amelioration.

CONCLUSION

I have proposed a way to improve your school. There is no perfect method for doing this. What I have suggested is an approach—called the ecological approach. I have set it forth in three phases, or stages. In the first, you try to create an open school—a school where all arrangements are open to criticism. In the second, critical dialogue phase, the authorities take the criticisms seriously when, through dialogue, they try to find out what specifically is wrong with the arrangements, or with the criticisms of them. In the third phase, experimentation, you modify or change the inadequate or harmful arrangements. The critical approach is a way to improve continually. So the new arrangements are also subject to criticism, critical dialogue, and experimental revision in light of unrefuted criticism.

The ecological approach is a human approach to improvement. By this I mean that it is a modest one, designed to human scale. It is not impositional: it does not have you telling others what a good school is. Rather, it constitutes a mutual quest to make your school better. It begins where you are, where the school is—with what exists. It is not dogmatic, but rather is in keeping with human fallibility.

Of course, it's not surefire. Nothing is.

NOTES

1. See, for example, Warren G. Bennis, Kenneth D. Benne, and Robert Chin, eds., *The Planning of Change* (New York: Holt, Rinehart and Winston, 1969), esp. part III; Matthew B. Miles, *Innovation in Education* (New York: Teachers

College Press, 1964), esp. part II; Goodwin Watson, ed., *Concepts for Social Change* (Washington, D.C.: Cooperative Project for Educational Development by National Training Laboratories, NEA, 1967); Seymour B. Sarason, *The Culture of the School and the Problem of Change* (Boston: Allyn and Bacon,1971); Neal Gross, Joseph B. Giaquinta, and Marilyn Bernstein, *Implementing Organizational Innovations* (New York: Basic Books, 1971).

2. See, for example, Jonathan Kozol, *Death at an Early Age* (Boston: Houghton Mifflin, 1967), and *Free Schools* (Boston: Houghton Mifflin, 1972); John Holt, *How Children Fail* (New York: Pitman Publishing, 1964), and *Freedom and Beyond* (New York: E. P. Dutton, 1972); George Dennison, *The Lives of Children* (New York: Random House, 1969).

CHAPTER 6

Skepticism and Schooling*

STEPHENIE G. EDGERTON

INTRODUCTION

In one of his *Sceptical Essays*,[1] Bertrand Russell discusses the role of social authorities in the goverance of education and the evils attendant on their misuse of power. Russell describes what he takes to be the viewpoint of the state, the church, school people, and parents on the ideal of education. He concludes that "no one of them may be trusted to care adequately for a child's welfare, since each wishes the child to minister to some end which has nothing to do with its own well-being." For Russell the maximum amount of authority in schooling should be the least authority. And the strongest argument for freedom, specifically freedom of opinion, is the doubtfulness of all of our beliefs.

Inadvertently, Russell raises for educators the simple but provoking question: "Should the schools be rooting *primarily* in various forms of faith?" I think they should not, for schooling which aims at overbelief too often leads to crude cynical perspectives

* This paper is published here for the first time. A version of this paper was read at the annual meeting of the American Educational Studies Association in Memphis, Tennessee, November 1976.

93

which form barriers to learning and promote antirational philoso-phies of confrontation. To avoid that kind of cynicism, what seems to be needed in schools today is a nonpsychological brand of skepticism. But let me attempt to spell out my case.

Russell challenges, quite rightly I think, the merit of asking children to subscribe without intellectual scrutiny to the educa-tional ideologies promulgated by social institutions. He sees the self-interests of these several social groups fostering perspectives of the "good life" which may indeed be incompatible with the indi-vidual's well-being. Raising the question, "What is the role of the school in society?" as Russell does, is fairly old hat. But arguing the case for his reply on the basis of the skeptic's viewpoint is unusual and would, I suppose, seem strange or at least impractical to most people. Pertinent as they may be, these abstract argu-ments addressing themselves, as they do, to problems of truth and credibility seldom hold credibility for even the highly schooled. This may result from educational experiences which are largely based on faith. Fundamentally, the great preponderance of schooling experiences issue a call for credibility. Acceptance of belief is the major goal. Analysis of argument is seldom heralded as a schooling outcome. How often do teachers ask students to do anything but believe?

RUSSELL'S SKEPTICISM

What is the skeptic's viewpoint? And why is Russell, at least in these essays, almost enamored of it? The standard formulation of skepticism says that there is no reason to believe one thing more than another. That is, there are no rational grounds for believing in one proposition over another. On this skeptical position, how-ever, one may nevertheless hold a belief on the basis of faith. Lacking rational grounds, one may commit oneself anyway.

Now, Russell's intellectual dilemma centered on what has been called the problem of induction. Following David Hume (1711–76), Russell concluded that the rational grounds for our knowl-edge claims had to rest on a faulty inductive logic. Unable to resolve the conflict between choosing rationally, which he defined as "empirically justifiable," or utilizing a logic which could not be justified, Russell opted to use the logic. The principle of inductive logic became for him a premise held on faith. Or, to put it another way, inductive logic is assumed in the process of choosing between knowledge claims.

As Russell well knew, such a state of affairs must cast doubt on our beliefs. And under these circumstances he is led to advocate the maximum amount of freedom while recognizing the need for some authority for children in school. The authority he recommends is the least authority.

PSYCHOLOGICAL SKEPTICISM

Not all forms of skepticism have taken the intellectual route Russell's did In the late sixteenth and early seventeenth centuries, for instance, skeptical arguments were used in a religious context to *defend* doctrines of faith as well as to attack them. These arguments, which centered on theological issues, are not widely known.[2]

There is, also, a modern secular version of skepticism which is of interest to school people. This view is held by neopragmatists. Its main spokesman was John Dewey. It suggests an ultrapsychological version of skepticism which concludes that all beliefs be held tentatively—subject to revision on the basis of new evidence. Action is prescribed, and it is action based on faith. Beliefs are warranted on the basis of one's feelings of confidence. The position in question, which frequently speaks in terms of statistical probabilities, calls for commitment. Since ultimately it bids us act on beliefs which have been internalized (they have become part of us, so to speak) and not upon propositions which we might test without believing them, it sets psychological limits to our opportunities for refuting or reinterpreting. There is considerable difference between a view that advocates acting on hypotheses and committing oneself to acceptance and socialization of their outcome and a view that advocates holding hypotheses as a source of tests without the need to ever believe in them. "Tentativity" is being defined quite differently.

To cast the matter a bit differently, this Deweyan formulation of skepticism would tend to render even more difficult the problem psychologists, social psychologists, and sociologists have repeatedly identified regarding attitudes. Attitudes, they tell us, are complex intellectual-emotional phenomena, extremely resistant to change. Or, as many reformers are heard to complain, "prejudice is nearly impossible of removal."

BELIEF MILLS WITH BUILT-IN PUNISHMENTS

When we define rationality in a psychological fashion, we substitute a psychological framework for a logical-empirical conceptual framework. This is most apparent when we use a psychological framework to view problems of schooling. This, perhaps, can best be seen by reviewing a series of transitions as they apply to classrooms envisioned with students and a teacher.

Note the psychological states in the second of each of these pairs:

Ideas become "self"
Competence becomes "perfection"
Errors become "failures"
Learning becomes "knowing"
Knowing becomes "conviction"
Decisions become "commitments"
Penalties become "punishment"
Criticism becomes "ridicule"

Children hold their ideas as part of themselves. They think that learning is knowing and believe that having competence is answering test questions and exercises perfectly. They hold their ideas with conviction and see intellectual decisions as a matter of commitment. When they make errors, they psychologize them into feelings of failure. As a result, children treat penalties as punishments, and any criticism of ideas becomes a case of ridicule. Another way of putting this is that intellectual work becomes ego involved and that changes of mind cause emotional stress.

Two anecdotal examples may assist in making this psychological emphasis clearer.

The ten-year-old daughter of a colleague of mine arrived home from school recently carrying her test paper. Embarrassedly, she pointed out the few items which had been scored wrong. Upon being queried, "Well, isn't that the way we learn—by making mistakes?" the young lady replied, "I thought it was the other way around."

Not long ago, my dinner partner, a bright and engaging young man of eleven, blurted out in a concerned and self-indicting manner, "I got three of them." Since I did not understand the context of his remark, I asked, "Three of them, three what's?" In much the tone of a confession, he replied, "Three D's."

These children are feeling and being punished by a psychologized orientation in schooling. Although it would appear otherwise, psychological versions of skepticism are psychologically self-defeating. In the end, an individual is being asked or being forced to become irrational in the name of rationality.

THE FALLEN FAITHFUL

But should the schools be rooted primarily in various forms of faith? Surely they should not if this leads to forms of disillusionment and cynicism at the private level and antirational ideologies at the public level. If those who head the educational establishment are unable to evolve institutions based on philosophies of education which offer logical-empirical dimensions of schooling that are compatible with the sociopsychological needs of human beings, they might expect a larger contingent of the fallen faithful. Students, that is, who are injured because of their faith.

But how might "the fallen faithful" be categorized? They can be seen, I think, as three groups: (1) there are those who believe and are ravaged psychologically; (2) there are those who no longer believe and are ravaged psychologically; and (3) there are those who are merely ravaged psychologically.

The subtlest tragedy can be attached to the first group. These are students who keep trying—not only trying to know but trying to believe. Many of them end up believing that they know; others end up believing that someone knows; still others end up wondering if there is anything to know. In each of these perspectives there is fertile ground for antirational development and pursuit of confrontation. Those who know are ready to lead. Those who know someone knows are looking for someone to follow. And those who wonder may already be disillusioned and bordering on severe cynicism.

What of those who no longer believe but are ravaged psychologically? These students may be thought of as the social realists. They discover early on that there is little reason to believe but through psychological pressures persist in the system. Many of these students feel forced to submit to the system; others feel forced to submit to the system while designing or searching for alternate systems; and still others feel there is no escape. Out of this group comes the more obvious forms of public cynicism—the first two hopeful and the last hopeless. This is all-too-apparent soil from which leaders and followers grow to engage in irrational confrontation.

The final group, those who are merely ravaged psychologically, are simply devastated.

There are, of course, those who escape all together. They are very few in number.

CONCLUSION

I have tried to argue that some forms of skepticism in schooling are very harmful. I hope I have pinpointed at least one variety, "psychological skepticism," as a particularly vicious approach. In its insistence on defining "rationality" in a sociopsychological manner, it creates a cruel atmosphere in classrooms and fosters unwarranted overbelief on the part of many students.

What tomorrow's schools need are institutions which represent an alternative theory of rationality that is more compatible with human needs. Following Sir Karl Popper, I think such a theory may be found in a form of sociological skepticism. This is an orientation which emphasizes fallibilism and our search for our mistakes. It asks that perspectives be held tentatively as searchlights in the pursuit of error. Students are asked to be critical of theoretical perspectives as well as to be critical of their own ideas. However, they are not encouraged to socialize or internalize these ideas. Rather, they are taught to utilize their ideas as interpretive vehicles. When interpretation fails, the students are urged to seek refined perspectives.

It could be said that this approach to rationality advocates intellectualization instead of socialization. It suggests that schools become places where students learn to interpret their world, not adjust to it. It emphasizes the limitation of our intellectual endeavors while insisting they be used wisely to scrutinize our environment.

NOTES

1. Bertrand Russell, *Sceptical Essays* (London: George Allen and Unwin Ltd., 1928). At this time I would like to acknowledge that I am indebted to critics who offered helpful suggestions: Professors Bernice Fisher, Ronald Swartz, and Mary Ann Raywid.

2. Richard H. Popkin, *The History of Scepticism* (New York: Harper and Row Torchbooks, 1964).

PART III

On Educational Innovations

CHAPTER 7

Education and the New Pluralism *

HENRY J. PERKINSON

THE EMERGENT NEW PLURALISM

My wife says it began about the time our son was born. Sam is now twelve years old. Others I've talked to date it from the assassination of John Kennedy. Some mark the Vietnam War as the start of it all. But, however people differ on the exact point when it began to change, everyone over thirty knows we are living in a new society, a society quite different from the one we all grew up in.

Many observers have characterized this new society by affixing the label "post": "postindustrial," "postliberal," "post-Christian," "postrationalist," and so forth. Yet, while it is true that the society we all knew has passed away, this obituary prefix fails to describe what is now aborning: the new pluralism.

---

* This paper previously appeared in *Journal of Thought* (November 1975), pp.293-303. The paper presented here contains a few minor changes from the original version.

Many people now accept, indeed seek, membership in the very groups they earlier tried to escape or even ignore. Psychologically minded observers see this as a quest for identity. I see it as an attempt to overcome powerlessness. Consciousness of victimization has driven people together, into groups of similarly situated "victims," forging them into "movements"—liberation movements. So today we have blacks and Indians, Italians and Mexicans, females and homosexuals, senior citizens and adolescents—all coming together, forming groups to combat the discrimination and oppression they endure. Slogans and epithets rain down on all sides: "Racist!" "Sexist!" "Honky!" "Male chauvinist!" (There is even the charge of "Speciesist!" leveled against those who discriminate against and oppress animals.) Organizations proliferate: Black Panthers, Gray Panthers, NOW. There is even an organization to protect ugly people—Uglies Unlimited—against discrimination by employers who advertise for "attractive" secretaries, hostesses, airline stewardesses, and the like.

This new pluralism extends beyond the traditional group lines of race, sex, ethnic origins, and age. For, while blacks, females, Italians, and senior citizens have all organized to protect themselves, others have done so, too, on different bases. This new pluralism, then, includes employees in the public service—policemen, fireman, sanitation workers, teachers, and public transportation workers—who have organized themselves into unions to protect themselves against exploitation; it includes consumers, who—rejecting the dictum caveat emptor—have organized into cooperatives, and into consumer groups to protect themselves against shoddy, unsafe, and defective merchandise; it includes the laity and lessery clergy who have organized to protect against the religious domination of the hierarchy; it includes prison inmates seeking to protect themselves against the dehumanizing prison system; it includes "concerned citizens" who have organized to get government out of the hands of the powerful special interests; it includes those seeking to protect a way of life, or a life-style—conservationists, hunters, hippies, pacificists, antinoise and antipollution groups; it also includes groups created for ad hoc protection against a specific threat—to save a tree from highway engineers, to protect a city block against crime, to preserve a historic landmark against demolition.

The most obvious consequences of this new pluralism is the overthrow of innumerable conventional mores. As different groups have coalesced and sought liberation, they have attacked and weakened long-accepted social restraints and restrictions. Divorce, abortion, pornography, even crime and incivility are but a few of the more dramatic social manifestations of battles against "victimization." No less dramatic are the changing behavior patterns in dress and speech: a new frankness, a deliberate flaunting of traditional prohibitions. In our public places and in our long-venerated institutions, customary decorum has disappeared: people no longer behave as they formerly did in churches, in schools, in courts, in the theater. Teachers, judges, clergymen, and political officials now experience a declining social authority; they no longer secure automatic respect.

This rapid and almost total overthrow of what many have long known, accepted, endorsed—and even revered—has caused much perplexity and dismay. There are widespread apocalyptic fears that civilization is ending. The schools, the churches, the family, the government—all seem to be falling apart.

Now, I rather doubt that civilization is falling apart (although it may be), but I do think that our social constructions—the ways we construe our social arrangements—are exploding. Indeed, our old constructions now seem quite simplistic. For a long time, we divided society into the poor and the rich, the liberals and the reactionaries, the altruists and the egoists. The first were the good guys; the second, bad guys. Now, because it is so wide, so broad, so deep, the new pluralism not only forces us to reconstrue good and bad; it also confronts us with the consciousness that each of us is simultaneously oppressor and oppressed. No matter who we are or what we are (and we are many things simultaneously—male or female; and adult or child; and white or black; and worker or employee; and consumer or merchandizer; and professional or client; and criminal or law-abiding citizen), we are a member of some groups which are oppressed, and at the same time, a member of other groups which oppress.

Our old, simplistic constructions of good guys and bad guys emerged from presumptions about what is "right," "true," "just," and "good"—for ourselves and others. According to those presumptions, it was "right" for whites to dictate how blacks should behave; it was "right" to determine their appropriate "place"; it was "good" to discourage and stamp out "unsavory" characteristics common to certain ethnic groups; and according to these presumptions, it was "true" that homosexuals are "sick," lawbreakers "belong in jail," and "a woman's place is in the home." Those presumptions led us to certain "just" expectations: elderly folks were supposed to retire peacefully and go live in St. Petersburg, or else be institutionalized; children should be seen (sometimes), but never heard—they ought to be confined in schools; and duly constituted officials of government were to be awarded respect, obedience, and deference: you *shouldn't* fight city hall.

But all these presumptions about what was "right" or "good" or "true" or "just" for different groups actually legitimatized oppression. This is not to say that members of certain groups were the victims of a conscious conspiracy on the part of other groups. It is just that these presumptions led us to construct arrangements in the society that have had unexpected implications and consequences which caused pain and suffering for some. And so long as it was assumed that the arrangements of the society were "right" and "proper," people concluded that the implications and the consequences were right and proper too—"That's life!"

Today, however, most of us have ceased to believe our social arrangements are correct. We no longer hold them sacred and immune from criticism. More and more, we now recognize that fallible men created the social arrangements we have, so they cannot be perfect. As a result, most of us are no longer willing to endure the pain and suffering these arrangements cause. People seek self-protection.

This concern with self-protection—the essence of the new pluralism—has revived a neo-Jeffersonian approach to society. As everyone knows, Jefferson thought that each person has an inalienable right to pursue happiness. To engage in such a pursuit, one must be free, and to remain free one has to be vigilant: the price of liberty is eternal vigilance. For Jefferson, permanent vigilance took the form of various institutionalized checks and restraints on those who would or might oppress others.

Today, people continue to insist—maybe more volubly than ever before—that each person has an inalienable right to pursue happiness. Concomitantly, each person still encounters many and various infringements of that right. In the past, many recognized that interference with their right to pursue happiness came about because they were members of some group: black, Italian, women, public employees, or whatever. And those who were victimized usually tried to escape (if they tried at all) by escaping from that group, or else they tried to demonstrate that they were a "different kind" of black, Italian, woman, public employee. But today, increasingly we witness battles for group liberty or freedom, group protests against discrimination and prejudice. What is new today is that these groups have become vigilant—many actually seem hostile and paranoid—in order to protect themselves.

Jefferson thought the government had the responsibility to secure the protection of the rights of every citizen, rights set forth in the Declaration of Independence and the Bill of Rights. Each could protect himself through using the arrangements institutionalized in the several branches of government. Today, we find groups using both governmental as well as extragovernmental means to protect themselves. Groups do use the courts, do lobby in the legislatures, and do appeal to government agencies to protect themselves. They engage in bloc voting during elections; they make and sign petitions, and they enact legally binding contracts and pacts. But they also employ boycotts, strikes, demonstrations, collective bargaining, confrontations, and dialogue; they use advertising and publicity and rely upon the media to expose those who threaten them. They create organizations that engender militancy; publish their own journals, magazines, and newspapers; and issue admonitory warnings to all would-be oppressors.

The new pluralism is expanding as more and different groups seek and secure their own self-protection. This improves society. On the one hand, it reduces the pain and suffering people have previously endured; on the other hand, it provides more people the freedom to pursue happiness in their own different ways. Of course, we shall never have a perfect society. The arrangements we construct will always be inadequate in some way; they will always cause some kind of pain and suffering. Yet, as our consciousness of actual pain and suffering expands, we can continually provide better protection for those who seek it. But there are limits here, too. Violence, terror, and revolution are not acceptable modes of self-protection. Recourse to them can destroy any society, especially a pluralistic one.

Now, if our society is to maintain and expand its pluralism—and thus becoming continually self-renewing—then it would help if all understand how its arrangements function, understand how groups have, can, and will protect themselves. With such knowledge and understanding, each person can then better exercise his right to pursue happiness and accept the rights of others to do likewise. We need an education designed to initiate people into the pluralistic way of life.

SCHOOLS AND PROTECTING SOCIETY FROM PEOPLE

Before investigating what might be an appropriate education for the pluralistic society emerging today, it might help to take a look at how our schools have functioned until now, how they have served the society.

Ever since first setting them up, we have used our public schools to combat pluralism. This becomes clear when we realize that the three periods of most intense concern about the workings of the schools took place at the very times Americans were trying to digest great numbers of immigrants. We have used the schools to absorb, assimilate, and integrate various different groups into the society. We have used them to transform and change people so that they would "fit in." We have used the public schools to unify, to solidify the society.

For the first two hundred years in the new world, Americans had no public schools of the type we know today. During this period, education here—as in Europe—was a private or philanthropic enterprise. Each family provided what it could for its own children, and voluntary agencies (especially churches), supplied charity education for the children of the poor. Then, in the first half of the nineteenth century, great numbers of immigrant Irish and Germans arrived. Crowded into the industrial and mill towns that were springing up throughout the Northeast, people blamed these "newcomers" for creating a host of social ills. "They" introduced crime, licentiousness, disease, corruption, and violence. Many began to fear for the stability of the society. The way to combat these ills, some argued, was education. As one social reformer put it: "They who refuse to train up children in the way they should go are training up incendiaries and madmen to destroy property and life, and to invade and pollute the sanctuaries of society."

But to secure education for all meant replacing the traditional private and philanthropic approach with a truly public one. At this point, reformers began to promote *public* schools—schools accessible to all, providing free education to all, and financially supported by all. According to Horace Mann, one of the most famous of these school promoters, education is "the great equalizer of the conditions of men, the balance wheel of the social machinery." Public schools, he promised, would dislodge and drive out "the great body of vices and crimes which now sadden and torment the community." The schools could pull this off through what was then called moral education: the development of self-discipline and habits of self-control. In America, the argument went, where people are free from surveillance and repression by church and state—so traditional in Europe—everyone had to be self-governing. Without self-control and self-imposed restraints, people—witness the immmigrants—would create chaos and anarchy.[1]

From its inception, then, Americans construed the public school as the agency to unify the society, to create social harmony and stability by imposing on all a common set of values, beliefs, and understandings.

Between 1890 and 1920 the United States received the greatest number of immigrants in its history. During this period, these newcomers—mostly from southern, central, and eastern Europe—settled for the most part in large cities. Here they joined others who had abandoned rural life in America. The rapid population explosion in the cities generated new social disorders and social ills. Once again, Americans turned to the schools.

This time, the task was overwhelming. By 1910 there were well over 9.5 million foreign-born in American cities, together with over 12 million natives of foreign or mixed parentage. Most were unskilled, unlettered, unwashed (literally), and unable to speak English. To assimilate these "foreigners," the city schools had to undergo a radical transformation. Teaching the traditional subject matter and trying to inculcate self-control were just not enough. The schools had to provide vocational training and training in homemaking skills; they had to wash and bathe children while teaching both young and old how to speak English as well as how to read and write it. Above all, the school had to teach cooperation and constructive social participation. In the words of one of the most famous architects of its transformation, the public school was to become "an embryonic community." In schools, the children were to learn how to live together in harmony. The school now deliberately made children conscious of their shared or common goals and taught them to work together to attain those goals. Through shared, common experiences, people of vastly different ethnic, religious, and social class backgrounds were to be transformed into a single community.

Of course, the public schools could not recapture and restore the face-to-face community that had existed before the rise of the cities. That had disappeared forever. But, by transforming itself into an "embryonic community," the schools could help to infuse the quality of cooperation and the procedures for securing consensus—both so necessary for creating and maintaining a unified, harmonious, and stable society. No one expressed this new conception more eloquently than John Dewey: "When the school introduces and trains each child of society into membership within such a little community, saturating him with the spirit of service, and providing him with the instruments of effective self-direction, we shall have the deepest and best guarantee of a larger society which is worthy, lovely, and harmonious." [2]

We are still in the midst of the third phase of intense educational activity—activity, like its predecessors, set afoot by a dramatic rise in the rate of immigration. During this third period of immigration, which began at the end of World War II, the migrants again flocked to the cities. This time, however, they came not from Europe but from this hemisphere: from Puerto Rico and the Caribbean, from Mexico, and from the rural areas of the South. Many spoke only Spanish; most were black or brown; all were poor. They swelled the "minority" population in every city; often their children became the majority in many city school systems.

Once again the rapid demographic changes in the urban areas of the nation created new, and intensified old, social ills and disorders. And once again people turned to the schools—to socialize the young, to integrate them into the larger society. To carry this out required large expenditures of money, time, and energy as new plans and programs came into being. Most of these experimental projects introduced into the urban schools were supposed to provide a "compensatory education" to help the minority children overcome their "cultural deprivation." Given a "head start," or initiated to "higher horizons," schoolmen expected the "minority group" children to be able to "keep up" and "move ahead" into the "mainstream of society." But, by the mid-1970s it became evident that the results had failed to live up to the expectations. The failure, some claimed, lay with the schoolmen themselves: they were prejudiced against minority children and had low expectations of their scholastic abilities. Moreover, the critics continued, this racism was built into the institutional arrangements of the school system itself. So, for education to work, much had to be changed: the patterns of control, the structure, the curriculum, the organization, even the personnel. Yet where these kinds of changes have taken place it is manifestly clear today that the schools have done little to assimilate the minorities.

Meanwhile, partly as a result of the schools' failure, a growing number of minority people began to reject the aim of integration into the mainstream of American society. Some noisily, others quietly, proclaimed, and thus quickened, a consciousness of group identity and feelings of racial and ethnic pride. They reconstrued assimilation as a covert form of group oppression. This became the source and inspiration for what I have called the new pluralism.

Once blacks and Spanish-speaking groups began to reject the schools' efforts to process them into "acceptable Americans," many demanded educational programs that would foster group pride and group identity. And so it happened that programs in black studies and Hispanic studies began to dot the educational landscape.

Recently, educators have become conscious of other cultural groups—Oriental, for example—who attend our urban schools. Might not they, too, have educational programs that preserve and extend *their* cultural heritage? This has resulted in a new movement that attracts many schoolmen: "Multicultural Education." The American Association of Colleges for Teacher Education (AACTE) has lately adopted a position statement, "No One Model American," produced by its own commission on multicultural education. That statement, in part, declares:

> Multicultural education rejects the view that schools should seek to melt away cultural differences or the view that schools should merely tolerate cultural pluralism. Instead, multicultural education affirms that schools should be oriented toward the cultural enrichment of all children and youth through programs rooted to the preservation and extension of cultural alternatives. Multicultural education recognizes cultural diversity as a fact of life in American society, and it affirms that this cultural diversity is a valuable resource that should be preserved and extended. It affirms that major education institutions should strive to preserve and enhance cultural pluralism.[3] ["No One Model American," *Journal of Teacher Education* (Winter 1973), p. 264]

This so clearly signals an advance over the traditional construction of schools as agencies to unify the members of all diverse groups into a homogeneous community that one hesitates to demur. Yet, I do think that it misconstrues what is happening in our society today and so fails to construct a more appropriate educational response. For, if my previous analysis is correct, we are in the presence of more than simply a renascent cultural pluralism. The pluralism emerging in our society is both broader and deeper. It encompasses sex, age, occupation, interests, abilities, as well as geographical location and physical and mental condition—to mention but a few of the bases already operative. People today are joining, or discovering themselves to be members of, groups distinguished by each of these characteristics.

Yet the members of these groups do not seek "the preservation and extension" of their differences. This is of no concern to women, consumers, or senior citizens, for example. Nor do the minority groups—blacks, the Spanish-speaking, or Orientals—strive to "preserve and extend" their differences. Some extremists—the nationalists—do. But when educators take their cues from them, they exacerbate dissension within our educational institutions. The result, predictably, is cultural conflict, usually sparked by disagreement over what is, and what is not, "truly" part of the culture that the school seeks to preserve and extend. And, understandably, protests arise that only bona fide members of that culture (black, Chicano, Puerto Rican, or whatever) can teach, administer, participate in, or evaluate the educational programs set up to preserve and extend the culture.

My objections to multicultural education are not solely directed to its divisive consequences. I object to the presumption the schools manifest in undertaking such an endeavor. As I understand it, the preservation and extension of one's inherited ethnic, racial, or cultural heritage is a private and personal matter, not one for the public schools. Many people do wish to identify themselves with this heritage; many seek to be free from it; others simply sustain a passive curiosity about it. So, just as people resented the earlier attempts of the schools to turn everyone into one model American, now many resent the attempt to type and enclose them, or their children, in a cultural, ethnic, or racial group. The old approach deracinated and deethnicized people, stripping them of their historical identity. It was impositional and authoritarian. But the new multicultural approach is impositional and authoritarian, too, even though in this case the identity the school wants to impose on each student is "his own." In both approaches, the school refuses to accept people as they are and as they want to be. It curtails the freedom of each person to pursue happiness in his own way.

If my previous analysis is correct, then, rather than "preserving and extending" their differences, what *every* member of a minority group wants is protection against victimization. This is what the new pluralism is all about. *Every* black, Puerto Rican, Oriental, in the United States—just as *every* woman, homosexual, adolescent, consumer, public employee—has suffered *some* kind of discrimination, affront, insult, or repression *because* of being a member of that group. But not just minority groups: every one of us belongs to many different groups; thus, every one of us is vulnerable to oppression from others. So, we are all interested in knowing how we can better protect ourselves. This, I think, is the appropriate social function for the school to take up in this age of new social pluralism.*

THE NEW PLURALISM AND THE SCHOOLS

To suggest that the schools should merely help people protect themselves cedes the schools a minimal social function. It is negative and passive, even static—quite unlike the dynamic, active, and positive tasks usually assigned to our schools. To accept it would signal a reduction of expectations about what schools can or should try to bring about. Instead of casting the school as the agency to create a new and better society by changing people, it construes the school as the agency that accepts people as they are and simply tries to help them better protect themselves, which means to help them secure the freedom necessary for them to pursue the kind of life they wish.

Actually, this suggestion for a minimal social function for the schools is not novel. It was the basis of the proposal for education in Virginia that Thomas Jefferson drew up in 1789. He proposed that all children should go to school for three years at public expense, there to be taught reading, writing, arithmetic, and history. Austere as it seems to us today, Jefferson thought that three years spent pursuing this simple curriculum would be sufficient to help people protect themselves. If everyone knew how to read and write so that they could use newspapers, and if all studied history so that they could spot tyranny in all its guises, then, he reasoned, people would be able to guard their own liberty.

---

* This is not to deny that schools have other functions in addition to the social function; e.g., intellectual functions, moral functions, economic functions, etc. See my *Possibilities of Error* (New York: David McKay, 1971).

Jefferson made his educational proposals in a time and place where the strains of social pluralism had not yet emerged, where differences of class and race, of ethnic origin, and religion were not threatening to rip apart the social fabric. When social pluralism did begin to emerge in the first half of the nineteenth century, many Americans feared it. Pluralism, they thought, could only produce anarchy and chaos. These fears lay behind the attempts to use the schools to contain and restrict blacks, ethnic groups, women, consumers, workers, and many others—socializing each group to fit into a society that had predetermined the ways the group could pursue happiness. Throughout their history, the public schools have functioned to protect the society *against* people— especially those people who, in one or another way, were *different*, and hence a threat to harmony and stability.

But today all about us we see a new social pluralism bursting forth. And though we experience uneasiness, tension, even conflict, there is no chaos, no anarchy—simply increased openness and freedom. In spite of long-standing dire fears to the contrary, most people *do not want to dominate others*. They merely want to be free to pursue happiness as they see fit, and they will go to great lengths to protect themselves so that they may do so.

Jefferson and others of the founding fathers recognized this human disposition, and as a result they charged social institutions—such as governments and schools—with the task of helping people peacefully protect this right to pursue happiness. Is it not time to restore this conception of what schools are for?

To carry out this minimal social function requires no great transformation of the schools. First, as Jefferson insisted, the schools should teach all to read and write. Literacy is a necessary qualification for self-protection. Beyond literacy, the burden will fall upon the teacher of social studies. Here, as with Jefferson's plan, teachers could stress the history of oppression. But whereas Jefferson limited this to the study of political and governmental oppression, today we would include studies of the various ways the many different groups have oppressed others: how whites oppressed blacks; men oppressed women; adults, adolescents; how manufacturers and merchandizers victimized consumers; employers, employees . . . and so on. Students could study how the victims became conscious of their oppression and how they constructed and used means of self-protection. In addition to history, students could learn what arrangements for self-protection presently exist and how these arrangements function.

But even beyond this history, I think social studies teachers will have to include instruction in the theory of self-protection. This social theory is at least as old as Jefferson. Let me remind you of some of its salient features by briefly sketching the principle, the focus, and the necessary precondition for its operation.

Beginning with the assumption that all people have the right to pursue happiness as they see fit, we can readily see that a perfect society cannot exist—simply because one person's pursuit may interfere with another's. This leads to the basic principle of accommodation: everyone should be able to protect himself.

The theory of self-protection focuses on the existing society. In it, various accommodations already operate through which people do protect themselves. But since we can never have a perfect society, the existing accommodations will always be inadequate in some way. Thus, all schemes for improving society will emerge from discoveries of existing inadequacies and will consist of refinements and changes in the arrangements to help people better protect themselves.

An open society is a precondition for self-protection to flourish. That is, the existing social arrangements must be open to criticism and refinable in light of unrefuted criticism. In an open society, people construe all existing arrangements as experiments that will, in time, and through criticism, reveal themselves as inadequate. Now, no society is completely open. Yet the logic of self-protection impels us to increase whatever openness there is, expanding the domain of criticism and critical dialogue so that more people can better protect themselves.

What results can we expect from this instruction in self-protection? The most significant one, I suggest, would be the emergence of a critical (or ecological) approach to society. The acceptance of a pluralistic society and the acceptance of the right of each group within that societal network to protect itself against victimization is tantamount to an ecological conception of social improvement. We here improve the society—as we improve the school (see chapter 5), and as we improve knowledge (see chapter 3): through criticism. With an ecological approach, we begin with the society as it now exists. Through criticism, we identify the evils within it: the adverse consequences for others of the behavior of one or more groups within the society. Then we try to modify that behavior so as to diminish or eliminate those adverse consequences. This improves the society.

To have a critical approach means to look out for oneself and to be receptive to others' attempts to do likewise. People would expect limits, boundaries, and restraints. But whenever they felt victimized by a specific restraint or oppressed by the acts of others exercising *their* right to pursue happiness, they would criticize, complain, and set about the task of better protecting themselves. To secure this, they would utilize the existing arrangements they learned about in school; they might, if necessary, try to create or devise new ones.

The emergent social pluralism in our present society condemns and rejects the traditional socialization function of the public schools. We no longer want schools that protect society *against* people; we want schools that protect people—or better still, schools that teach people how to protect themselves.

NOTES

1. Horace Mann, "Tenth Annual Report," in *Life and Works of Horace Mann* 5 volumes, edited by Mary Peabody Mann. (Boston, 1891). See also "First Annual Report," and "Horace Mann" in my *The Hundred Years of American Educational Thought* (New York: David McKay, 1976).

2. John Dewey, *The School and Society* (Chicago: The University of Chicago Press, 1900) p. 44.

3. "No One Model American," *Journal of Teacher Education*, (Winter, 1973) p. 264.

CHAPTER 8

Induction, Skepticism, and Refutation: Learning Through Criticism *

STEPHENIE G. EDGERTON

INTRODUCTION

Quite by accident one evening while reading I found an interesting example of what might be interpreted as a "reading" problem. Let me relate the story to you, for among other reasons it may serve as a source of comfort when you face, as many of you do daily, the enormously complex and difficult task of trying to teach students of the social studies to read. I happen to have found the incident very exciting, for it stimulated thought about the reading process; and I am hopeful that in sharing it with you I may assist you in your quest to develop better readers.

* The major influences on this paper are the studies of Karl R. Popper in logic and scientific methodology. J. Agassi, B. Fisher, H. J. Perkinson and Ronald Swartz offered helpful comments and criticisms. The paper previously appeared in *A New Look at Reading in the Social Studies*, edited by Ralph C. Preston, (International Reading Association, Newark, Delaware, 1968-69), pp. 60-69.

WHEN DISTINGUISHED PHILOSOPHERS READ

Some years ago the philosopher Paul Arthur Schilpp began editing a series of books called the *Library of Living Philosophers*. The general idea of the series was to present an opportunity for philosophers to discuss the work of an eminent "living" philosopher by offering comments and criticisms on which this philosopher would then write comments in reply. The format for each volume included a brief intellectual autobiography, approximately twenty papers, and a response to these papers. One such volume had as its subject the philosophy of Bertrand Russell.

The perspectives of Bertrand Russell are known to many people in many walks of life. Russell has been vigorous as a disputant concerned with a wide range of social issues. His more academic interests have focused on the foundations of mathematics, the methodology of science, the constructions of language, and the workings of the human mind. Young philosophers, typically, are introduced to his work early in their schooling, at which time they are told of his unusual lucidity. In the minds of most philosophers, Russell's clarity of expression enjoys competition only with the clarity of his famous friend and philosopher, G. E. Moore.

But an interesting thing occurred on the occasion of the Schilpp-Russell volume. Schilpp reports in the way of apology to the distinguished philosophers who wrote papers for the volume— no doubt after thorough study of the Russellian writings on the topics of their contributions— and to the future readers of the books that the brevity of Russell's replies are to his mind explained by a comment made by Russell to the editor in private conversation. Russell disclosed to Schilpp his surprise in finding after careful reading of the manuscripts of the twenty-one contributors that "over half of their authors had *not* understood" him. Schilpp tells us that "This fact amazed Mr. Russell all the more because he always thought that he had been making every effort to write clearly and to express his ideas in the briefest possible and most direct way." [1]

The question I wish to raise is: How could this happen? How may we explain the failure of a number of distinguished philosophers to interpret with some degree of accuracy and appreciation the thought of another very distinguished philosopher renowned for his clarity of expression? And how could it be that men of superior competence in matters of logic, semantics, and epistemology—disciplines from which other scholars draw their rules of critical thinking and,[2] more recently, critical reading [3]—have difficulty reading critically? Are the problems of interpretation related to matters of logic? of semantics? of epistemology? and, if they are, in what ways?

I seem to have stumbled across a very interesting example, one which I would like to explore philosophically. In this case, playing the role of a philosophical explorer means playing the game of a theoretical capitalist. Theoretical explorations of this kind, of course, unlike those of such well-known adventurers as Sir Edmund Hillary, who as you recall has provided us with magnificent accounts of his mountain-climbing and polar expeditions,[4] have wide latitude for error. Indeed, from my point of view, intellectual expeditions may profit greatly from bold conjecturing, followed by determined and deliberate quests for error.

From the outset it should be understood, then, that I do not wish to claim for my remarks the fruits of the experimentalist. That is, the systematic testing of theories is not my forte. Those who engage in such activities will be the subject of my opening remarks.

MAN THE THEORETICIAN

Psychologists, sociologists, anthropologists, social psychologists, among others, have been working for many decades to discover and test theoretical information bearing on the problems of how people learn, think, perceive, and so forth. Unfortunate as it may be, the fact remains that to date we have no "mindoscopes." We do not know, as a matter of fact, how people learn or how people think; nor do we know how many ways people may learn or people may think. As brilliant and informative as are the theoretical contributions of such great social scientists as Freud, Malinowski, Marx, Skinner, and Piaget, to name a few, our theoretical poverty about people is fairly staggering.

Perhaps no one suffers more from this social scientific void than members of the teaching profession. They are regularly asked to accomplish feats of "teaching-learning" with little or no assistance from science. That they have done as well as they have seems, at least to me, a tribute to their own theoretical talents, though admittedly most teachers do not see themselves as theoreticians.

Seeing oneself as a theoretician is helpful, I think, in understanding why even distinguished philosophers have difficulty reading the lucid Bertrand Russell. I wish to suggest that *man is a theoretical animal*, bringing to his reading his theories, his perspectives, his viewpoints, or his biases in the light of which he attempts to interpret the theories of other men. This is no small achievement, as I hope my example indicates.

The problem seems to be one of utilizing one's own theoretical frameworks to discover the theoretical frameworks of another. We seem to approach the written word with bundles of theoretical materials—generalizations at many levels of abstraction on various topics—from which we then select, in hope of discovering the theoretical underpinnings or assumptions of an author's prose. If we are lucky, the writer may state his problem for us, feed us cues, and offer us forms of rhetoric and other devices which will help us to select the *theoretical arenas* in which we may through trial and error cull and create theoretical statements which seem fitting as an interpretation.

When we have what seems to be a match between his theoretical frameworks and ours, we seem to need some form of feedback to check it out. While reading a book, paper, or whatever, the interaction is limited substantially between the author and us in such a way that we, as readers, must do most of the work. All we seem able to do is to look for cues which indicate that our interpretation is inconsistent with what the author says. Finding such a cue, we may alter our theoretically constructed interpretation to take account of it. In the situation of schooling, we may, of course, introduce a mediator into the process—a teacher. The teacher may assist the reader by raising questions which lead to the digging out of cues, which in turn stimulate the reconstruction of an interpretation. Advanced readers, like the distinguished philosophers, may play each of the roles themselves. And, presumably, beginning readers may learn to become advanced readers. Part of advancing one's reading acumen, if I am right, is the recognition that the reader and the read both come with perspectives.

Let me briefly analyze my intellectual activities of the past two paragraphs. What I seem to have offered are psychological and sociological speculations about the act of interpretation when reading. I talked about operations of the mind, a reconstruction of an author's viewpoint, and a form of group interaction. I made hypotheses—offered theories—about what may happen in a situation when one is reading or learning to read well. Interestingly, my activity parallels in some respects the work of many theorists of curriculum and instruction. Much of what happens when designing teaching-learning units seems to qualify as sociological activity—specifically, applied sociology. Psychological considerations are no doubt implicit, in the sense of theories of mind, in these processes. This analysis tempts me to suggest that educational researchers confound logic and psychology while doing a form of sociology. If this is the case, theorists of curriculum and instruction might be wise to look over the various schools of sociology for assistance in what they are doing.

My speculative comments apart, it is unfortunate that the psychological and sociological processes of interpretation still remain secrets to us. This condition should not, however, move us to treat them as if they were not; or to treat them as if they were something else. Borrowing ready-made solutions to problems may, if we are not careful, get us into trouble. A case in point would be an adoption of the Baconian tradition of inductive scientific methodology as a learning technique.[5] But let me make myself clear.

Speaking forcefully against human prejudice, Sir Francis Bacon outlined a methodology of knowledge gathering designed to eliminate human error. But in the designing, Bacon seems to have eliminated too much. Seeing man as the holder and creator of *false* theories, he expelled from scientific activity man the theoretician. Eager to remove error from our scientific investigations, he lost sight of our greatest potential for knowledge—the creative powers of human beings. He traded a most imposing scientific resource, men's minds, for one of the products of their genius—a seemingly foolproof *logic of inquiry.* And I wish to stress that this exchange was done in the name of the doctrine of "pure" objectivity, which was, incidentally, a prejudice of his own.

Bacon did not see that the question of how and where we get our ideas is different from and must be separated from the question of how we evaluate them. When we do not make the distinction between the *origins or sources* of our theories and *evaluations* of them,[6] we shortchange ourselves in terms of viewing man's creative potentials. At the same time, we support barriers and erect blockades to an adequate analysis of the processes of inquiry. A glaring example of this confusion is the refusal by many to accept "intuition" as a source of theoretical information. Interestingly, this old and venerable notion has recently come into its own in the description scientists and those who study the activities of scientists give us.[7]

The inadequacies of our sociopsychological theoretical explanations which are related to the problem of interpretation must not, on the other hand, prohibit us from guessing at the solutions to the problem. Indeed, offering bold conjectures seems to be the way of the scientist. That he plays many roles—logician, mathematician, experimentalist, educator—should not allow us to overlook his role as theoretical speculator struggling to learn from experience. Though as yet he has given us little in the way of help in the form of theoretical information concerning problems of learning to read *well,* he has offered us, indirectly, a model for learning. He has offered himself, the scientist, as an exemplar.

But to take him as our model necessitates in many cases a revision of our notions about him. Unlike the Baconian version,[8] this suggestion asks for the recognition of the scientist as a creative man—as an *abstractor* instead of an *extractor.*[9] It says that, as man the theoretician, he comes to his work with his theories and he creates theories. Although the scientist as depositary and creator has been played down in the descriptive literature, logic and discretion tell us that it is precisely because he comes with something that he can hope to refine it; we cannot refine what we do not have.

The main thesis, then, of this paper is that man the discoverer, man the creator, man the theoretician takes what he has, juggles it, twists it, pulls it, and adds to it—sometimes through rearrangement—making interpretation possible.

Taken seriously in the context of reading—especially with the new trend to place rich theoretical information further and further down in the grades—the notion that man is a theoretician means encouraging readers to *boldly conjecture,* to *guess.* As teachers, it means asking students to prize themselves, not as empty storage bins, but as theoreticians. To follow such a prescription will increase the incidence of error. It implies that we learn by *making* mistakes. It suggests that teachers help students to become *courageous readers,*[10] readers who are willing to risk mistakes and, going even further, students who are willing to search out their own errors while humbly admitting man's fallibility in the pursuit of learning.[11]

Of course, there are those who may say that to allow students to think, to wildly guess, may have its dangers. After all, encouragement in the direction I am suggesting may lead to students' prizing their own theories too highly. Like some people whom all of us have known, they may behave, when they first encounter their own ideas, as if this were the first time mankind had ever had them. As offensive as this consequence may seem to some, it tells us that we need to help students to learn *much more. We need to assist them, for example, in learning to discriminate between questions of originality* (when, how, and with whom an idea was original) and questions of *status* (whether or not an idea is a "good" one, given the job we want it to do and how we may set about to evaluate it—whoever its inventor).

LEARNING ABOUT LOGIC AND EXPERIMENTALISM

Asking students to recognize themselves as theoreticians seems to suggest helping them, also, to become logicians and experimentalists. Once students begin to pay attention to their own theories, they will need to find ways to sort them out and to test them. Perforce, they will need to consider, even *as* theoreticians, the problems associated with the quest for knowledge. Questions they might entertain are: How may we learn from experience? How may we choose hypotheses? How may we validate theory? This is to say that students should be urged to consider the logic of inquiry.

Were teachers to open this world, students would fast discern how tools of *deductive* logic may be utilized to delineate their speculations in such a way that setting up experiments becomes conceivable. Inventing procedures for testing, when seen as a theoretical activity reserved for the imagination, may become exciting.

Learning to read well seems to be no exception. The exceptional reader like those distinguished philosophers of whom Russell did *not* complain, to my way of thinking, is a person who is unafraid of his imagination and unafraid of making errors. He is a reader who recognizes ways in which evaluative techniques, such as our evolving rules of logic and methodology, may assist him in garnering interpretations. He does, indeed, want to appreciate the thought of others and actively seeks to come to an understanding of their perspectives and insights—ever aware that their thought, like his, is human and subject to mistakes.

Pioneers in the quest to teach children the use of logic have been many. Teaching children to do so in the circumstances of reading has come to be labeled by educational theorists and researchers "critical" reading.[12] Taking their cues from those who have attempted to make analyses of what would constitute "critical thinking," [13] researchers have developed descriptions and exercises whereby teachers might teach and children might learn to make logical and empirical judgments about nonfictional writings.

As important as these contributions have been, they may be, I think, improved through criticism. Let me offer two examples. The first will focus on a situation in which children are taught to judge the warrant of generalizations susceptible to action. The second will focus on teaching children the use of credentials to judge the alleged authority of an expert.

Teaching children rules, through the application of which they may ascertain the reliability of generalizations, hypotheses, conjectures (or systems thereof), is to teach children a methodology of belief. It is to teach them an answer to the question, "How do we know what to believe?" Through the collection of positive cases, children will learn which generalizations are worthy of their belief. In other words, they will learn a means of deciding which generalizations they should act upon. But such generalizations, carrying (at least for children) a high probability of success, quite frankly, may carry a "higher probability" of failure. The reason for this apparent double-talk is fairly simple: gross assumptions yield gross predictions. Without highly accurate theoretical information about the behavior of people, generalizations about contemplated actions run a high possibility of error. Even attempts to minimize risk are undercut by the absence of social scientific theory which approximates the truth.

Disillusionment and skepticism may be the outcomes of teaching children to rely on rules of logic which incorporate gross procedures for success.[14] When children discover that generalizations gathered from data collection do not work, they may question not only those who teach them the procedures of reasonableness but *reason* itself.

Were this questioning to lead to improved rules for the assessment of hypotheses and not the tragic consequences I have sketched, it would, indeed, constitute a revolution in schooling. It would introduce into our schools the notion that scholars, teachers, and students learn by making mistakes. An innovation of this kind would bring with it the further prescriptions: "Make mistakes as fast as you can! And remember them!"

Turning to my second example, children may be taught to look up the background or credentials of a writer as an aid to interpreting his work. If children are aware that authors present in their writing their viewpoints or perspectives, they may learn to use information about the author's field, his training, other works he has written, those he footnotes, and so on, as cues for ascertaining his viewpoint. They may, for instance, make hypotheses about the kinds of problems in which scholars or a given discipline are interested and ask of their reading whether these or similar problems are the concern of the author. They may ask whether the problem to which he addresses himself in this work assumes the solution of other problems discussed in his other writings.

What children should *not* be taught is to utilize the credentials of a writer as *some form of guarantee* for his ideas. No matter how many degrees he may hold, how many books he may have written, how high the esteem in which he is held, his theories or ideas (or portions thereof) may be in error. Although an author may be offering the reader the latest word, *his* latest word, it should *not* be treated as if it were some *guaranteed* word or the *last* word.

While I would opt for the use of logic to assist students in judging the validity of an alleged authority's argument, I would also advocate that students be given assistance in learning to play the role of the experimentalist. Teachers could help students to make attempts to determine whether an authority's statements are empirically testable and, if so, in what ways.

Contriving experimental procedures which count as crucial tests (cases in which there is a strong possibility of refutation) could only broaden a student's perspective of knowledge and the problems associated with its growth. Students should come to see how conflicting viewpoints or theories (if you prefer) aid us in uncovering explanatory deficiencies. Specifically, considering two conflicting theories intended to explain the same phenomenon, they might note observations disclosed by one theory which its competitor must also explain or be labeled deficient. Exploring the subtleties of experimental procedure, they could come to understand "why" statistical generalizations leave room for improvement; to date, we have no adequate means for refuting them.[15] When we calculate the probabilities of a state of affairs, we are going for the second prize; from the beginning we have admitted that a number of cases will not fall under the *affirmative* scope of our generalization. It is at the point of application that "reason" must come into the picture.

One lesson of "reason" is learning that knowledge, like the people who create it, as well as the processes they create for its evaluation, is *human*. And I can think of no lesson more important to learn or more important to teach. Were educators interested in the social studies to assist the young in learning this lesson, such educators would be far on the way toward shaping a *creative-rational citizenry*.

APPENDIX: THE LOGIC OF INDUCTION

Some among each generation of young philosophers take as their challenge the resolution of the logical problem of induction. These empiricists attempt to find new ways to overcome the skepticism borne of David Hume's (1711-76) articulation of the dilemma involved in attempting to demonstrate through experience the truth of universal statements. Since universal propositions refer to tomorrow's (infinite) states of affairs, they must refer to unexaminable phenomena—making *complete* empirical demonstration impossible.[16] This logical difficulty has vexed, perennially, those who would have science be a system of demonstrably true laws.

A number of approaches have been taken to resolve the empiricists' problem of unjustified inference, that is, reasoning from the examined to the unexaminable.[17] By far the greatest number of efforts have aimed at crawling over Hume's argument, usually attempting to show its inapplicability. Philosophers of science, in general, have held high hope that Hume was wrong. How else could we explain the unprecedented achievement of science?

The contemporary logician, Sir Karl Popper, has taken a novel approach. Following in the tradition of Immanuel Kant (1724-04), Popper has accepted what he calls Hume's "logical discovery that induction is irrational." [18] However, he has abandoned, even attacked with logical and empirical arguments,[19] Hume's *psychological* thesis that people do and must methodologically induct. Popper points out that the *acquisition of ideas* is a subject for scientific investigation, not a matter of scientific methodology.

Unlike Bertrand Russell, a deductivist who saw a need for inductive inference, Popper has offered a deductive methodology which avoids inductive inference.[20] Specifically, it avoids probabilistic and verficationist reasoning. Deductive methodology for Popper amounts to deductive logic (reasoning from the general to the specific) plus negative testing procedures (logical and empirical refutations).

From Popper's standpoint, a body of scientific knowledge may never be demonstrated. Science is a series of *guesses* or *conjectures* which are the result of attempts to formulate and answer scientific problems.[21] They are, indeed, guesses and conjectures which have withstood our severest attempts to refute them. But they may never be said to hold greater status—for they are *only man's best approximation* of the truth. Although we may never know the truth, we *may know* what is *not* the truth.

This, it would seem, is a very optimistic viewpoint, for man's *more* creative approximations may lie just around the corner. In fastening on negative experimentalism, efficiency in the growth of knowledge is enhanced. In separating the psychology and sociology of knowledge from its logic and testing, all avenues of acquisition are opened to man's creativity and study.

Popper's studies in logic raise many significant and sticky questions for educators interested in the social studies. Among them are the following:

1. May we be said to be "certain" about theoretical knowledge in any but the psychological sense that some people feel certain about its truth?
2. If a number of men agree, after careful study of the evidence, that a statement is true, is their judgment only as "good" as their inductive theory of rationality on which it is based?
3. Should "security" in the classroom ever reside, however indirectly, in the knowledge discussed there?
4. Is there a "structure of knowledge" in any sense, save that the formulation of problems is a selection device for the discovery of their solutions?
5. Do theories of induction by repetition and elimination qualify mainly as theories for the inculcation of knowledge?

NOTES

1. Paul Arthur Schilpp, ed., *The Philosophy of Bertrand Russell*, vol. 1 (New York: Harper and Row, 1966), vii–viii.
2. Robert H. Ennis, "A Concept of Critical Thinking," *Harvard Educational Review* 32 (Winter 1962): 81–111.

3. Martha L. King, Bernice D. Ellinger, and Willavene Wolf, eds., *Critical Reading* (Philadelphia: Lippincott, 1967).

4. Edmund Hillary, *High Adventure* (New York: E. P. Dutton, 1955), and *No Latitude for Error* (New York: E. P. Dutton, 1961).

5. Chapter 1 of this volume.

6. Karl R. Popper, *Conjectures and Refutations: The Growth of Scientific Knowledge* (New York: Basic Books, 1963).

7. Michael Polanyi, *Personal Knowledge: Towards a Post-Critical Philosophy*, rev. ed. (New York: Harper and Row, 1964); *The Tacit Dimension* (London: Routledge and Kegan Paul, 1966); Karl R. Popper, *Conjectures and Refutations, The Logic of Scientific Discovery*, English edition (New York: Basic Books, 1959); Calvin W. Taylor and Frank Barron, eds., *Scientific Creativity* (New York: Wiley, 1963).

8. Chapter 1 of this volume.

9. Joseph Agassi, "The Novelty of Popper's Philosophy of Science," *International Philosophical Quarterly* 8 (September 1968): 442–463.

10. B. E. Cullinan proposed this descriptive label in a private conversation.

11. Henry J. Perkinson, "Fallibilism as a Theory of Instruction," *School Review* (forthcoming).

12. King, Ellinger, and Wolf, Eds., *Critical Reading*.

13. Robert H. Ennis, "A Definition of Critical Thinking," *Reading Teacher* 17 (May 1964): 599–611.

14. Stephenie G. Edgerton, "Have We Really Talked Enough about Authority?" *Studies in Philosophy and Education* 6, no. 4 (Spring 1969); 275–77.

15. S. Korner, ed., *Observation and Interpretation in the Philosophy of Physics* (New York: Dover Publications, 1962, and Imre Lakatos, ed., *The Problem of Inductive Logic* (Amsterdam: North-Holland, 1968).

16. Chapter 1 of this volume.

17. Lakatos, Ed., *The Problem of Inductive Logic*.

18. Ibid.

19. Popper, *Conjectures and Refutations*.

20. Popper, *The Logic of Scientific Discovery*.

21. Joseph Agassi, *The Continuing Revolution* (New York: McGraw-Hill, 1968).

CHAPTER 9

Authority, Responsibility, and Democratic Schooling*

RONALD M. SWARTZ

I am a democrat because I believe that no man or group of men is good enough to be trusted with uncontrolled power over others. And the higher the pretensions of such power, the more dangerous I think it both to the rulers and to the subjects.

—C. S. Lewis

THE EDUCATIONAL PROBLEM OF DEMOCRACY

In an ideal democratic community all individuals have the opportunity to participate in making major decisions that can affect their lives. Although it is wrong to assume that individuals will always make correct decisions, democratic societies are based on

---

* This essay previously appeared in *The Cutting Edge* (Spring 1976), pp. 8–19. The paper presented here contains a few minor changes from the original version.

the notion that it is better to give a little authority and responsibility to many people rather than to place a great deal of authority
and responsibility in the hands of a few individuals.

Unfortunately, democratic communities are not social pana-
ceas; like all human groups, democratic ones can act irresponsibly
and can at times misuse authority. One of the ironies of a democracy is that decisions based upon majority rule can take away, as
well as protect, individual rights and liberties; the establishment
of democratic procedures merely implies that a group has decided
on a *means* of making decisions. And democratic societies often
attempt to achieve different ends and goals.[1] What distinguishes
democracies from other groups is that the decision-making process
can be influenced by many different individuals.

In this chapter I would like to discuss some issues associated
with having schools that are run as democratic communities; a
school that is a democratic society is one which establishes procedures and policies that make it possible for all school members
to partake in making major decisions that will affect what goes on
in the school.[2] Later I will make concrete recommendations about
how a school might become a working democracy, but here I wish
to state that my aim is not to discuss the many different aspects of
democratic schooling in general. In this paper my discussion is
centered around the question, "How might authority and responsibility be viewed and used in democratic and nondemocratic
schools?" This question, which I will refer to as the *educational
problem of democracy,* is the central concern of this essay.

Although I will discuss many issues associated with the educational problem of democracy, I do wish to note that, unlike many
other contemporary educators who are interested in the relationship between schooling and democracy, my aim here is not to
discuss the question, "What should be taught in schools that exist
in democratic societies?" Rather than being concerned with issues
related to the development of the "proper" curriculum for schools
in a democracy, this essay will discuss issues associated with creating schools that are run as democratic communities.[3]

OVERVIEW OF THE ARGUMENT

My plan is to discuss two major solutions to the educational problem of democracy. The first solution is what I refer to as a *conventional view of schooling.* According to this view, people claim that there are some authorities that can be consistently relied upon to be responsible for determining and controlling school activities. In contrast to the conventional outlook, I will consider a *liberal view of schooling.* This view claims that the responsibility for determining school activities should not be placed in the hands of a few chosen authorities which have been socially certified as "reliable." The arguments throughout this paper assume and suggest that the liberal view of schooling is more satisfactory than the conventional view.

These two views of schooling are often connected with educational programs that have the potential to lead either to democratic or to nondemocratic schools. As we will see, the conventional view of schooling is closely associated with nondemocratic educational programs, which do not endorse the notion that all individuals should be seen as social, political, and intellectual equals within the context of a school. In contrast, the liberal view of schooling is consistent with democratic learning.

Much of what I will say about authority, responsibility, liberalism, and democratic schooling restates some of the ideas developed by such figures as John Stuart Mill, Bertrand Russell, Karl Popper, F. A. Hayek, Charles S. Peirce, Paul Goodman, A. S. Neill, Homer Lane, and others. Although I do not agree with everything these thinkers have said, my arguments rely to a great extent on what they have written about authority and schooling. However, my aim is not merely to restate the theoretical ideas these writers have developed, but to interpret their ideas and draw educational implications from them. In addition, my goal is as practical as it is theoretical, because I explain how different notions about democracy can influence educational practices. Unfortunately, when philosophers of education deal with such abstract ideas as democracy and authority, there appears to be—and at times is—no connection between theory and practice. In this paper

I try to bridge the gap between theory and practice: I intend to make concrete suggestions about the kinds of educational policies that are consistent with both liberal and conventional views of learning environments.

A RECENT DEFENSE OF CONVENTIONAL SCHOOLING

A major distinction between democratic and nondemocratic schools is that the democratic schools allow all school members to check and criticize those who are placed in positions of authority and responsibility. Many educational programs in our society are nondemocratic and authoritarian in essence because they do not provide individual school members with effective ways to check the authority of teachers, curriculum developers, school administrators, and the like.[4]

It is not uncommon for educators to ask students and nonprofessionals to place their faith in those who have been socially and officially certified as reliable authorities; pleas of this kind are often vague and ambiguous. However, this lack of clarity has been avoided in the recent work of Dr. Kenneth R. Conklin.[5] In one of his latest essays, Conklin states:

> Education cannot properly function in a democratic way . . . students must have faith and trust in their teacher. . . . Within the classroom a teacher must be the master of curriculum and classroom management.[6]

Dr. Conklin is a very recent, highly articulate spokesman for the conventional view of schooling. Conklin views professional educators such as teachers and curriculum developers as authorities who can be, and at times are perfect. One indication that Conklin thinks that teachers are perfect is his claim that they at times know the "truth":

> Teachers and students do not function as a voluntary community of co-learners or truth seekers, but as . . . judges and judged.[7]

Dr. Conklin seems to be suggesting that teachers should be viewed as reliable authorities who are at times perfect (i.e., they know the truth about issues related to the subjects in which they have been trained). Conklin does not claim that the "truths" known to teachers can be easily communicated to their students; rather, he endorses a principle of ineffability which claims that people cannot verbally communicate truth.[8] Conklin's notions about ineffability are some of his most interesting ideas; they are also the part of his philosophy that I consider to be the most dangerous—dangerous because they suggest that school members should have a blind faith in those people who have been placed in positions of authority and responsibility.

One of the most disturbing aspects of this educational philosophy is that it does not take into account the possibility that those in power might be mistaken in their judgments about what ideas are true; nor does it allow for the possibility that those in power may be incompetent or untrustworthy. All he can tell us is that:

> In view of the impossibility of expressing absolute knowledge, and the inappropriateness of dogmatism, we may rest more easily in recalling the authority of trust, charisma, tradition, example, and communities of persuasion.[9]

I find this assertion most distressing: all of the authorities Conklin cites are highly questionable at best. When one considers relying on the authority of tradition, for example, one cannot help but recall the many centuries in which people relied on the authority of the Aristotelian tradition, which, among other since discredited notions, claimed that the earth was in the center of the universe. In addition, reliance on such "authorities" as charisma may easily lead to tyranny and other disastrous social consequences. All charismatic people are not necessarily benevolent; the charisma of Adolf Hitler, for example, resulted in death and disaster for millions of people and irrevocably altered the course of modern history.

It is, of course, somewhat unfair to talk about Hitler's charisma in relationship to what Conklin meant when he said that we could rest more easily on the authority of charisma. Conklin was certainly not condoning, and I am sure he would not condone, the atrocities committed in Nazi Germany. When Conklin speaks about relying on the authority of charisma, he has in mind such benevolent people as Socrates and the Buddha.[10] However, what needs to be noted is that men like Hitler have been charismatic for large numbers of people.

WESTERN EDUCATIONAL THOUGHT; EXPERTS AS AUTHORITIES

Although Dr. Conklin's ideas deserve to be discussed on their own merits, I do not intend to provide a systematic criticism of his views here. I have singled out Conklin's work as a concrete example of a contemporary educator who argues against democratic schooling. Furthermore, Conklin's work is a good illustration of the fact that democratic schools are far from our educational norm. In many ways, Conklin's essays offer a justification for the status quo in education. Of course, Conklin's rationale for the kinds of schools that presently exist in our society may be somewhat different from other justifications, and he should be admired for his clarity and straightforwardness. Nevertheless, he can be seen as one of the many Western educational theorists who have suggested and assumed that it is a mistake to create democratic schools.

A historical survey of the different intellectual traditions in Western thought is beyond the scope of this essay, but such a survey might reveal that Western educational thinking has been greatly influenced by nondemocratic ideas. Such great Western educational theorists as Plato and Rousseau either knowingly or unknowingly at times assumed that it was a mistake to run schools as democratic communities.[11] It is interesting to note that even Rousseau, who is often viewed as a champion of student rights and libertarian educational programs, could not strip teachers of the responsibility of controlling the educational process of the young. Although Rousseau did not recommend that teachers overtly control classroom activities, he did see teachers as people who should manipulate the learning situation in order to control what students learn. As Rousseau once said:

It will probably be necessary to give him [the student] a little guidance. But let it be very little, and avoid the appearance of it . . . at most, arrange some practical situation which will make him realize things personally.[12]

What I wish to point out with respect to this passage is that the notion of giving adults the responsibility of controlling school activities may appear in the most unlikely places. Many Western educational theorists, both before and after Rousseau, have in some form or another endorsed the following educational policy: teachers, school administrators, curriculum developers, child psychologists, parents, and other socially certified experts are reliable authorities who should determine and control what students learn and do in the classroom.[13] I refer to this statement as *the policy of expert authority;* a school that endorses this policy will be referred to as a conventional school.

The policy of expert authority is a partial answer to the question, "Which authorities should be responsible for deciding and determining school activities and policies?" This question can be labeled *the educational problem of responsibility.* In addition, it is often tacitly assumed that the policy of expert authority is so reasonable that it does not have to be clearly stated or argued for; many people simply assume that it is natural for adults to control the educational process of the young. An interesting aspect of Dr. Conklin's work is that it attempts to justify policies such as the one on expert authority.[14] Unfortunately, educators do not usually argue for this policy; it is more common merely to accept it as both reasonable and desirable.

I believe that the policy of expert authority should be rejected because it makes the unreasonable claim that some people can be viewed as consistently reliable authorities. One lesson that can be learned from such libertarian political and philosophical theorists as Mill, Russell, and Popper is that no authority can be consistently relied upon. The reasons for rejecting policies such as the one on expert authority are manifold and detailed. Briefly stated, this policy is unreasonable because there is no way to satisfactorily demonstrate that any authority is infallible and consistently reliable.[15] As the libertarian political theorists have pointed out, all attempts to demonstrate the reliability of any authority must lead to circular arguments, contradictory arguments, or an infinite regress.[16] Furthermore, the libertarian political theorists have suggested that even if people think they have discovered an authority that appears to be infallible today, there is no way to guarantee that this "superauthority" will be infallible tomorrow. The future may not, and often does not, repeat the past.[17]

PERSONAL RESPONSIBILITY AND SELF-GOVERNING SCHOOLS

In order to thoroughly discuss the arguments in favor of, and those against, the policy of expert authority, it is necessary to consider many theoretical ideas about authority, responsibility, and schooling. I do not wish to treat all of these theoretical arguments; instead, I wish to discuss a solution to the educational problem of responsibility that is consistent with the development of democratic schools. A point that should be stressed about the policy of expert authority is that it provides the basis for nondemocratic educational programs. If people wish to have democratic learning situations, then they will have to find alternatives to the policy of expert authority.

One educational policy that seems to be consistent with the creation of democratic schools is what I refer to as *the policy of personal responsibility*. This policy can be formulated by the following statement: all school members, including students, should be viewed as fallible authorities who are personally responsible for making decisions about their school activities and many of the policies that govern a school; educational programs that endorse this policy can be referred to as self-governing schools.[18]

Policies such as that of personal responsibility may foster many different kinds of consequences. The actual empirical consequences associated with this policy cannot be easily identified; it will probably take much time and many social experiments before we learn more about this policy. However, an interesting consequence I associate with the policy of personal responsibility is that it provides the potential to create democratic learning environments. That is, in self-governing schools all individuals are viewed as fallible authorities who can influence, and at times greatly control, what happens in their school and lives.

We have much to learn about democratic educational programs such as self-governing schools. However, a fact worth emphasizing is that these schools do not eliminate the idea of having school authorities. Self-governing schools allow for the creation of some authorities; a major difference between democratic and non-democratic schools is that the former give school members the opportunity to check and criticize the authorities to whom people appeal. In a very real sense, the policy of personal responsibility makes every school member an authority within the school. When an educational program endorses such a policy, each individual is viewed as an authority who can participate in making decisions about school activities and policies. Nevertheless, self-governing schools do not assume that all school members are reliable authorities; consequently, it is possible to have authorities such as school rules that check the authority of the individual. Self-governing schools are not lawless places where people can do anything they wish, whenever they wish, because the authority of the individual can be checked by such authorities as the laws of the school or of society.[19]

As with the policy of expert authority, that on personal responsibility has its historical roots in Western thought. In fact, the policy of personal responsibility is an outgrowth of liberal philosophical, political, and educational thinking. Although most liberal thinkers have not attempted to apply their political and philosophical ideas to the educational process, the policy of personal responsibility relies to a great extent on what liberals have said about authority, responsibility, and democracy; a historical account of the ideas associated with self-governing schools would probably reveal that these schools are not totally foreign to Western society. It is interesting to note that the teaching method Plato attributed to Socrates in *The Apology* seems to suggest that Socrates would be somewhat sympathetic to democratic schooling.[20] Since Plato's ideas developed and changed throughout his life, it is possible to claim that his work contains ideas that can be associated with both democratic and nondemocratic schools.[21]

The history of democratic schooling is a fascinating subject and needs to be further researched. However, proper limits of this essay do not permit delving extensively into history, and I would like to conclude this brief introduction to self-governing schools with the following three points: (1) the dominant educational institutions in Western societies have not usually endorsed such policies as that of personal responsibility; (2) in those societies where self-governing schools have existed, they have generally been few in number compared with schools that endorse some version of the policy of expert authority; and (3) a school such as Summerhill, which was founded in England over fifty years ago by A. S. Neill, can be seen as a contemporary example of an educational program that endorses some variation of the policy of personal responsibility.[22]

PRACTICES IN CONVENTIONAL AND SELF-GOVERNING SCHOOLS

I stated earlier that an aim of this essay is to discuss some of the practical implications of different views of authority, and I would now like to discuss the fact that educational practices in conventional schools are very different from those in self-governing schools. In order to make my discussion of educational practices somewhat manageable, I have decided to center in on two major areas of an educational program. These two areas are: (1) student-teacher relations and (2) curriculum development. For the remainder of this essay I will discuss these two educational variables with the aim of demonstrating that conventional and self-governing schools lead to very different educational practices.

STUDENT-TEACHER RELATIONSHIPS

One of the glaring differences between democratic and non-democratic schools is that the students and teacher in these two educational settings have very different kinds of relationships with each other. Most of us have gone to conventional schools where the policy of expert authority was either openly or tacitly endorsed. In these schools a person often gets the message that teachers are very special people; teachers in conventional class-

rooms can rightly be viewed as special because their job is to decide, determine, and control the school activities and behaviors of
students. Since teachers in conventional schools are certified as
reliable educational experts and authorities, they are allowed to
tell students what do do; those students who disobey, or disagree
with, the teacher's dictates have no recourse except to yield to the
teacher's desires or be punished.

What I am asserting here is that in conventional schools the
relationship between students and teachers is not one between
equals but is greatly skewed to the teacher's advantage. In conventional classrooms the teacher's dictates and desires often have the
force of law, because students do not have the means to challenge
a teacher's views.[23] Put another way, the relationship between students and teachers in a conventional school is based upon a lop-
sided power distribution which places the teacher in a position to
control and determine what students do.[24]

I see no need to describe the relationship between students and
teachers in conventional classrooms at greater length. My guess is
that many of us have at one time or another experienced the
frustrations that go with being at the mercy of our teachers; the
policy of expert authority is so well accepted in our society that it
is almost impossible to avoid some contact with schools that endorse this policy. The policy of expert authority is often a part of
educational programs from kindergarten through graduate school.
Furthermore, although most teachers do indeed tend to be somewhat benevolent, it is likely that even the most obedient students
will at times feel that their teachers are making unreasonable demands. Of course, students will not always be justified holding
such views, but in conventional schools students do not normally
get a chance to air their views in a meaningful way. Instead of
openly confronting their teachers in order to iron out disagreements, students in conventional classrooms often resort to devious
and indirect ways of dealing with a teacher's demands.[25]

In self-governing schools the relationship between students and
teachers is very different from that found in the conventional
schools. One of the most significant educational consequences of
the policy of personal responsibility is that it makes students and
teachers political equals within the context of a school; that is, the

power relationship in democratic schools is such that students have the right to question a teacher's judgments. Thus, students in self-governing schools are not at the mercy of their teachers; they can speak their minds and criticize a teacher's views. In broader terms, all the people in self-governing schools have the opportunity to have some degree of control over what goes on during their school day.

As noted earlier, Summerhill is a contemporary example of a self-governing school, and it exists without making any political distinction between students and teachers; at Summerhill all school members have the same amount of power to influence the determination of school rules and activities.[26] There is another way to envision the political equality that exists in self-governing schools: each person has one vote in all matters related to the organization and running of the school. And as has been noted, all members of self-governing schools have the power to greatly determine their own school activities, and no individual must blindly do as someone else wishes.

It is an error to assume that an equal power relationship between students and teachers means that adults will never be able to influence what happens in a school. Most self-governing schools do allow adults to become members, and the adults in these schools can, like all other individuals, speak their minds. Although the power and authority given to adults in self-governing schools is much less than that of teachers in conventional schools, adults have not been stripped of all their influence and thus can affect what goes on in the school. If we assume that the percentage of adults in self-governing schools will be the same as, or higher than, the percentage of adults in conventional schools, then these few adults could use their power to help children create a meaningful and worthwhile democratic educational environment. It would probably be impossible for one hundred six-year-olds to start their own self-governing school; these schools should and usually do include people from many different age groups.

By no means do the few existing self-governing schools prove that democratic schooling is workable under all circumstances and for all people. Nevertheless, despite our lack of knowledge about these schools, they do pose a significant challenge to our traditional notions about the relationship that should exist between students and teachers. These few self-governing schools enable us to understand that it is important to ask questions such as, "Should we create more schools where students and teachers are viewed as political equals?"

CURRICULUM DEVELOPMENT

Democratic and nondemocratic schools also have very different notions about how to develop a curriculum. In a conventional school there is usually a standardized curriculum which every student must in some sense attempt to learn. This standardized curriculum is determined by adults, and students have very little say about what should be learned in school. Of course, most teachers try their utmost to make the standardized curriculum as interesting as possible.[27] Also, in our best conventional schools students are allowed to learn the curriculum at their own individual pace.[28] However, student input into what is included in the curriculum is minimal or nonexistent.

Self-governing schools totally do away with the notion of the standardized curriculum.[29] In these schools all individuals are responsible for making their own curricula, since there is no school authority who decides what is worthwhile to learn. Nevertheless, as noted in the previous section, adults in self-governing schools can and should make recommendations to students. Although the adults in these schools do not determine school activities, they can attempt to help students learn how to develop and sustain interests.

In considering how teachers in self-governing schools can help students develop a curriculum, I would like to briefly describe a pedagogic technique that may prove useful to members of self-governing schools. The pedagogic technique I have in mind can be referred to as a problem-solving approach to the development of interests. By means of this approach, people try to articulate the questions that interest them, and they also try to learn about all the different possible answers to their questions.[30]

The problem-solving approach that I am endorsing here is somewhat different from other such approaches that have been developed for conventional schools, because I am not suggesting that a school certify certain problems as worthy of being worked on. Nor am I suggesting that a school try to teach or convince children to believe in particular answers to questions. I am saying that problems can help people expand and pursue their interests simply because questions are a workable, efficient way for people to organize and study different points of view.

One of the most interesting aspects about questions and problems is that they are linguistic expressions that allow us always to consider at least two different points of view. This is of course obvious if we reflect on what questions are. However, many traditional educational programs have used questions as a way to teach children the proper and correct ideas to know and believe.[31] Programs that use questions in this way do not allow individuals to develop their own curriculum; instead, they try to convince children to accept only those ideas that the school and the society view as worthy of knowing. Nevertheless, problems can be studied as open-ended situations which have a variety of related solutions and arguments. Thus, one way to acquire a built-in mechanism for expanding interests is to ask questions. Once a question is articulated, people are in an excellent position to develop their interests because they can study various and different points of view. This historical and sociological approach to problem solving provides a wealth of information that will allow one's interests to expand rather than stagnate.

Learning how to expand interests and how to relate these interests to the rest of the world is not a problem that is unique for members of self-governing schools. This problem exists for most people. Much of what I have said about problem solving can be used in almost any educational program. However, in order to be compatible with the policy of personal responsibility, a problem-solving approach must do at least the following: (1) allow students to study questions they consider to be interesting and important; and (2) allow students to study problems so that they are not expected to "discover" or believe particular answers to questions.

CONCLUDING REMARKS

A major point I have been leading up to in the previous two sections is that self-governing schools allow students and teachers to engage in a creative dialogue over educational issues. Although it has not been possible here to describe in detail all the many ramifications of a policy such as that of personal responsibility, I have attempted to demonstrate that self-governing schools represent a viable educational alternative. It is my hope that the arguments presented here will help others realize the need to create more self-governing schools. In my view, the creation of self-governing schools should be seen as an immediate goal of educational reform. Nevertheless, it would probably be a mistake to create many of these schools all at once. Since self-governing schools may eventually totally reconstruct and otherwise change our notions about what schools should do, it is probably wiser to begin the reconstruction of schooling with some well-planned pilot programs. Hopefully, these pilot programs will become a beginning effort to improve our notions about schooling.

NOTES

1. For a classic statement about how majority rule can be misused in a democratic society see John Stuart Mill, *Considerations on Representative Government* (Indianapolis: Bobbs-Merrill Company, 1958), pp. 102–26. Also, for a more recent discussion about how majority rule can lead to different kinds of societal goals see Friedrich A. Hayek, *The Constitution of Liberty* (Chicago: Henry Regnery, 1960), pp. 103–17.

2. A discussion of some of my earlier ideas on democratic schooling can be found in the following: Ronald Swartz, "Education as Entertainment and Irresponsibility in the Classroom," *Science Education* 58, no. 1 January–March 1974): 119–25; "Some Criticisms of the Distribution of Authority in the Classroom," *Focus on Learning* 4, no. 1 (Spring–Summer 1974): 33–40; and "Schooling and Responsibility," *Science Education* 59, no. 3 (July–September 1975): 409–23.

3. The issues and questions associated with developing curriculum designs for schools in democratic societies are discussed in the following: Jerome Bruner, *The Process of Education* (New York: Vintage Books, 1960), p. 1; Harry S. Broudy, B. Othanel Smith, and Joe R. Burnett, *Democracy and Excellence in American Secondary Education* (Chicago: Rand McNally, 1965). It is interesting

146   ON EDUCATIONAL INNOVATIONS

to note that despite their concern with curriculum development in democratic societies, many contemporary educators have not seriously dealt with questions related to making schools working democracies. For examples of educators who have considered the possibility of having democratic schools see A. S. Neill, *Summerhill* (New York: Hart, 1960), pp. 45–55; Paul Goodman, *Compulsory Mis-education and the Community of Scholars* (New York: Vintage Books, 1960), pp. 43–48.

4. See the references in note 2. In addition, for an explanation about why it is desirable for democratic communities to check all authorities see Karl R. Popper, *The Open Society and Its Enemies*, vol. 1 (New York: Harper and Row, 1962), pp. 120–37. For a discussion about the need to check the authorities used in an educational program see Bertrand Russell, *Sceptical Essays* (New York: Barnes and Noble, 1961), pp. 127–38. Also, for information about the need to set bounds on the authorities used in an educational program see Richard Peters, *Authority, Responsibility, and Education* (New York: Erikson-Taplinger, 1960), pp. 13–24. Finally, see C. S. Lewis, *Of Other Worlds* (New York: Harcourt, Brace and World, 1966), p. 81. It should be noted here that the epigraph at the beginning of this essay comes from this last reference.

5. For an introduction to Conklin's work see the following: Kenneth R. Conklin, "Developmental Psychology vs. the Open Classroom," *Educational Forum* 39, no. 1 (November 1974): 43–47; "Knowledge, Proof, and Ineffability in Teaching," *Educational Theory* 24, no. 1 (Winter 1974): 61–67; "Due Process in Grading: Bias and Authority," *School Review* 81, no. 1 (November 1972): 85–95; "Fallibilism: A Terrible Mistake," *Educational Forum* 36, no. 1 (November 1971): 35–42; "A Defense of the Teacher as Taskmaster (Choreographer of Student Learning)," *Science Education* 59, no. 1 (January–March 1975): 107–11. In this last article Conklin criticizes some of the ideas I developed in "Education as Entertainment and Irresponsibility in the Classroom." In part, this present essay is an attempt to answer some of the criticisms that Conklin has offered for my ideas on authority and education. For a summary of how I view the debate between Conklin and myself see Swartz, "Schooling and Responsibility," pp. 409–12. Finally, I would like to thank Dr. Conklin for commenting on an earlier draft of this paper. Although he does not endorse the arguments in this paper, he has been kind enough to try to help me better understand the issues that interest us.

6. Conklin, "Knowledge, Proof, and Ineffability in Teaching," p. 66.

7. Conklin, "Due Process in Grading: Bias and Authority," p. 95. Also, for an interesting discussion which tries to explain why a teacher's knowledge is not perfect see Stephenie G. Edgerton, "Have We Really Talked Enough about Authority?" *Studies in Philosophy and Education* 6, no. 4 (Spring 1969): 369–83.

8. Conklin, "Knowledge, Proof, and Ineffability in Teaching," p. 64.

9. Ibid., p. 65.

10. This interpretation of Conklin's ideas has been confirmed in private conversations and letters. Although I do not claim to be an expert on Conklin's private thoughts, I do think he has had only the best of intentions. I believe that

Conklin has gone astray because he does not realize that malevolent people will at times be viewed by some people as benevolent authorities.

11. For a statement by Plato which seems to indicate that he does not endorse the notion of having democratic schools see Plato, *The Republic of Plato*, trans. F. M. Cornford (New York: Oxford University Press, 1965), p. 69. Also, see notes 12, 20, and 21.

12. Jean Jacques Rousseau, *The "Emile" of Jean-Jacques Rousseau*, trans. and ed. William Boyd (New York: Teachers College Press, 1967), p. 76. In addition, for a recent attempt to relate some of Rousseau's ideas on authority to the development of an educational program see David Bricker, "Rousseau's *Emile*: Blueprint for School Reform?" *Teachers College Record* 74, no. 4 (May 1973): 537–46.

13. See the references in note 2.

14. See the reference in note 5.

15. For a good summary of the arguments associated with viewing all authorities as fallible see John Stuart Mill, *On Liberty* (Middlesex, England: Penguin Books, 1974), pp. 75–86. For a recent discussion about how Mill's ideas relate to the development of educational programs see Kenneth A. Strike, "Philosophical Reflections on Tinker vs. Desmoines," *Philosophy of Education 1974: Proceedings of the Thirtieth Annual Meeting of the Philosophy of Education Society*, ed. Michael J. Parsons (Edwardsville, Ill.: Philosophy of Education Society, 1974), pp. 397–410. It is interesting to note that Strike argues along with Mill that many of the ideas associated with liberalism should not be applied to children and schooling. However, one of the significant assumptions of my essay is that liberals have been far too reluctant to apply their ideas to educational programs. As I see matters, the arguments for liberty and democracy are as valid for children as they are for adults.

16. A summary of some of the arguments related to viewing authorities as fallible can be found in Charles Sanders Peirce, "The Scientific Attitude and Fallibilism," *Philosophical Writings of Peirce*, ed. Justus Buchler (New York: Dover Publications, 1955), pp. 42–59. Also see *Karl R. Popper, Conjectures and Refutations: The Growth of Scientific Knowledge*, (New York: Basic Books, 1962), pp. 3–30. Finally, see the references in note 4.

17. The arguments related to the notion that the future may not necessarily repeat the past are an application of some of David Hume's ideas on experience and induction.

18. Refer to note 2 and the last two references in note 3.

19. For a discussion on how self-governing schools do indeed provide for ways to check the authority of individual school members see Neill, *Summerhill*, pp. 45–55.

20. See Plato, *Euthyphro, Apology, Crito* (Indianapolis: Bobbs-Merrill, 1956), pp. 39–41. In addition, a contemporary interpretation of Socrates' views on authority and responsibility can be found in Popper, *The Open Society and Its Enemies*, vol. 1, pp. 169–201.

21. The democratic and nondemocratic ideas in Plato's works are discussed in

Thomas Landon Thorson, ed., *Plato: Totalitarian or Democrat?* (Englewood Cliffs, N.J.: Prentice-Hall, 1963). Also, see Bertrand Russell, *A History of Western Philosophy* (New York: Simon and Schuster, 1945), pp. 82-108. Finally, see the last reference in note 20.

22. Refer to notes 2 and 19.

23. Refer to notes 6, 7, and 9.

24. See Swartz, "Some Criticisms of the Distribution of Authority in the Classroom," pp. 33-40.

25. See Swartz, "Education as Entertainment and Irresponsibility in the Classroom," pp. 120-22.

26. Refer to note 19.

27. Refer to note 25.

28. For an example of a contemporary educator who tries to foster individuality in the sense of having people learn the same skills and ideas at their own pace see Alexander Frazier, "Individualized Instruction," *Change and Innovation in Elementary and Secondary Organization,* ed. Maurie Hillson and Ronald T. Hyman (New York: Holt, Rinehart and Winston, 1971), pp. 217-28. This article is highly representative of the way individuality is often viewed in contemporary educational circles. It should be noted that self-governing schools need to be disassociated from this view of individuality because these schools do not make any systematic curriculum demands on students.

29. See the references in notes 2, 19, and 28.

30. The problem approach to learning that I am suggesting here has been discussed throughout the work of Karl R. Popper. For a summary of some of Popper's main ideas about problems see Karl R. Popper, *Objective Knowledge* (London: Oxford University Press, 1972), pp. 153-90. Also, see Ronald Swartz, "Problems and Their Possible Uses in Educational Programs," *Philosophy of Education 1973: Proceedings of the Twenty-ninth Annual Meeting of the Philosophy of Education Society,* ed. Brian Crittenden (Edwardsville, Ill.: Philosophy of Education Society, 1973), pp. 135-45.

31. See Swartz, "Problems and Their Possible Uses in Educational Programs," pp. 137-38.

Index

149

φ   062MµL

          SWARTZ